DIGITAL COLLECTIONS AND EXHIBITS

Library Technology Essentials

About the Series

The **Library Technology Essentials** series helps librarians utilize today's hottest new technologies as well as ready themselves for tomorrow's. The series features titles that cover the A–Z of how to leverage the latest and most cutting-edge technologies and trends to deliver new library services.

Today's forward-thinking libraries are responding to changes in information consumption, new technological advancements, and growing user expectations by devising groundbreaking ways to remain relevant in a rapidly changing digital world. This collection of primers guides libraries along the path to innovation through step-by-step instruction. Written by the field's top experts, these handbooks serve as the ultimate gateway to the newest and most promising emerging technology trends. Filled with practical advice and projects for libraries to implement right now, these books inspire readers to start leveraging these new techniques and tools today.

About the Series Editor

Ellyssa Kroski is the Director of Information Technology at the New York Law Institute as well as an award-winning editor and author of 22 books including *Law Librarianship in the Digital Age* for which she won the AALL's 2014 Joseph L. Andrews Legal Literature Award. Her ten-book technology series, The Tech Set, won the ALA's Best Book in Library Literature Award in 2011. She is a librarian, an adjunct faculty member at Pratt Institute, and an international conference speaker. She speaks at several conferences a year, mainly about new tech trends, digital strategy, and libraries.

Titles in the Series

1. *Wearable Technology: Smart Watches to Google Glass for Libraries* by Tom Bruno
2. *MOOCs and Libraries* by Kyle K. Courtney
3. *Free Technology for Libraries* by Amy Deschenes
4. *Makerspaces in Libraries* by Theresa Willingham and Jeroen De Boer
5. *Knowledge Management for Libraries* by Valerie Forrestal
6. *WordPress for Libraries* by Chad Haefele
7. *Game It Up!: Using Gamification to Incentivize Your Library* by David Folmar
8. *Data Visualizations and Infographics* by Sarah K. C. Mauldin
9. *Mobile Social Marketing in Libraries* by Samantha C. Helmick
10. *Digital Collections and Exhibits* by Juan Denzer
11. *Using Tablets and Apps in Libraries* by Elizabeth Willse
12. *Responsive Web Design in Practice* by Jason A. Clark

DIGITAL COLLECTIONS AND EXHIBITS

Juan Denzer

ROWMAN & LITTLEFIELD
Lanham • Boulder • New York • London

Published by Rowman & Littlefield
A wholly owned subsidiary of The Rowman & Littlefield Publishing Group, Inc.
4501 Forbes Boulevard, Suite 200, Lanham, Maryland 20706
www.rowman.com

Unit A, Whitacre Mews, 26-34 Stannary Street, London SE11 4AB

British Library Cataloguing in Publication Information Available

Library of Congress Cataloging-in-Publication Data

Denzer, Juan, 1972–
Digital collections and exhibits / Juan Denzer.
pages cm. – (Library technology essentials ; 10)
Includes bibliographical references and index.
ISBN 978-1-4422-4374-3 (cloth : alk. paper) – ISBN 978-1-4422-4375-0 (pbk. : alk. paper) – ISBN 978-1-4422-4376-7 (ebook)
1. Library exhibits–Technological innovations. 2. Libraries–Information technology. 3. Museum exhibits–Technological innovations. 4. Museums–Information technology. I. Title.
Z717.D39 2015
025.042–dc23
2015013749

∞ ™ The paper used in this publication meets the minimum requirements of American National Standard for Information Sciences Permanence of Paper for Printed Library Materials, ANSI/NISO Z39.48-1992.

Printed in the United States of America

In memory of my father, who taught me how to overcome obstacles with a little ingenuity.

CONTENTS

SERIES EDITOR'S FOREWORD

Libraries are exploring many new and exciting ways to exhibit their special collections, both in the physical library space and digitally on the Web. *Digital Collections and Exhibits* is an essential resource that examines just that. This one-stop reference manual identifies what it takes to produce an out-of-this-world digital exhibit including an in-depth discussion of tools and techniques, a look at how other libraries are building cutting-edge digital exhibits, and an analysis of what's on the horizon. Author Juan Denzer expertly guides the reader from planning to implementation of these stunning museum-quality interactive digital exhibits, including how to create hands-free exhibits with Microsoft Kinect, how to create exhibits using Open Exhibits, and even how to create 3D objects for online exhibits.

The idea for the "Library Technology Essentials" book series came about because there have been many drastic changes in information consumption, new technological advancements, and growing user expectations over the past few years that forward-thinking libraries are responding to by devising groundbreaking ways to remain relevant in a rapidly changing digital world. I saw a need for a practical set of guidebooks that libraries could use to inform themselves about how to stay on the cutting edge by implementing new programs, services, and technologies to match their patrons' expectations.

Libraries today are embracing new and emerging technologies, transforming themselves into community hubs and places of co-creation through makerspaces, developing information commons spaces, and even taking on new roles and formats, all the while searching for ways to decrease budget lines, add value, and prove the return on investment of the library. The "Library Technology Essentials" series is a collection of primers to guide libraries along the path to innovation through step-by-step instruction. Written by the field's top experts, these handbooks are meant to serve as the ultimate gateway to the newest and most promising emerging technology trends. Filled with practical advice and project ideas for libraries to implement right now, these books will hopefully inspire readers to start leveraging these new techniques and tools today.

Each book follows the same format and outline, guiding the reader through the A-Z of how to leverage the latest and most cutting-edge technologies and trends to deliver new library services. The "Projects" chapter comprises the largest portion of the books, providing library initiatives that can be implemented by both beginner and advanced readers, accommodating for all audiences and levels of technical expertise. These projects and programs range from the basic "How to Circulate Wearable Technology in Your Library" and "How to Host a FIRST Robotics Team at the Library" to intermediate such as "How to Create a Hands-Free Digital Exhibit Showcase with Microsoft Kinect" to the more advanced options such as "Implementing a Scalable E-Resources Management System" and "How to Gamify Library Orientation for Patrons with a Top Down Video Game." Readers of all skill levels will find something of interest in these books.

In 2014, at the Computers in Libraries conference, Juan Denzer presented "'Kinect'-ing Patrons to Experience Digital Collections," which illustrated the ways libraries could hack the Microsoft Kinect to create interactive digital exhibits, create 3D image objects from books, and build virtual reality reading kiosks, and it was the most innovative approach to digital exhibits I had ever seen. After that, I knew he needed to write down everything he knew about digital exhibits and collections for the rest of us. Librarians who are considering how to "wow" their patrons with their special collections won't want to miss this one.

—Ellyssa Kroski
Director of Information Technology
The New York Law Institute

http://www.ellyssakroski.com
http://ccgclibraries.com
ellyssakroski@yahoo.com

PREFACE

Computers have evolved from terminals that display plain text to flat panels displaying images, text, and sound. Users are able to interact with these displays using touch, sound, and hands-free motions. And libraries are taking advantage of these cutting-edge technologies in this exciting digital age. They are designing amazing exhibits using everything from simple computer hardware to advanced technologies such as the Microsoft Kinect.

Libraries of all types are looking to add new experiences for their patrons through these exciting new digital exhibits. The problem for many, however, is where to start. Where can librarians find a place to begin that they can use as a reference with actual projects? This book offers that help. I will walk you through a collection of easy-to-follow projects that any library can implement. And you will gain the knowledge and confidence to create and design your very own stunning digital exhibits.

ORGANIZATION AND AUDIENCE

Digital Collections and Exhibits is a how-to book designed to take away the mystery of digital exhibits. Unlike other how-to books, this book is written for every type of learner; for those who want to read it in order from the first chapter to the last, or for those who want to dive right in and skip ahead to the Projects chapter. Each chapter complements the others, but you can feel free to jump from chapter to chapter.

Chapter 1 provides background information as well as details about the importance of digital exhibits. It gives you a brief overview of the significance of the projects and why they were chosen. Chapter 2 discusses topics for getting started. It includes a discussion of copyright issues, location, budgets, and project selection. Chapter 3 provides carefully selected tools and applications. Each one is explained in detail, which will help you understand how it will be useful. Chapter 4 profiles other libraries that have designed digital exhibits. The case studies are there to help you see how others have created some very exciting exhibits and to provide inspiration. Chapter 5 is the Projects section. The Projects will range from easy to moderate. Every project is detailed so that anyone can implement it. Chapter 6, the "Tips and Tricks" chapter, provides the best practices and tips to maintain your digital exhibit. Chapter 7 discusses the future trends and directions this field is taking. It includes information on upcoming trends and exciting new technologies that may someday be used in digital exhibits. Finally, the book includes a list of recommended reading, chock-full of resources to help you further empower yourself with skills to create even more exciting digital collections and exhibits.

Librarians often come to me with ideas for projects. They tend to begin a conversation with "I saw this . . . is it possible?" or "Can we do this?" My response always begins with "If they can do it, so can we." *Digital Collections and Exhibits* was written to give you the power to say "If they can do it, so can we."

ACKNOWLEDGMENTS

The world of libraries is a place I never thought I would end up in. I have to thank Tom Tran, my colleague and friend, for that. When others were unsure whether to give an out-of-work system administrator/programmer a chance, Tom knew how hard it was to look for a job in this economy. He convinced them to give me shot, which changed my life for the better.

I also want to thank all of the people I work with at Binghamton University Libraries. For me, every day there is a pleasure from the time I step into the library to the time I step out. You are my extended family.

Thank you to my colleague Ben Andrus, who may not understand the exact details of how some technology works, but he sure understands the importance of it and where to apply it. When others were not sure whether to support my ideas, Ben always saw the potential. It is his support that led to getting this book published.

Thanks also to our former dean of libraries John Meador, who gave me the nickname "Magic Juan." It was his support of my ideas that drove me to be more dedicated to my career and work.

And of course thank you to Mien Wong, my colleague, coinventor, and friend. I spend most of my time thinking logically and approaching things systematically. She helps me by taking that robotic thinking in me outside the box and letting my creative side run free.

I cannot thank Ellyssa Kroski enough. She recognized the passion I have for this profession and gave me the change to be heard. Her patience with me and push to keep me going are truly her greatest strengths.

Finally, I want to thank my family, friends, and Maggie, who always was excited to hear my progress. Above all, thank you to Christine, who is my true friend; she has been there for me when I needed someone the most. I owe my success to her.

1

AN INTRODUCTION TO DIGITAL COLLECTIONS AND EXHIBITS

Digital technology that uses multimedia has been around since the 1990s. The term *multimedia* has become so common that it is rarely used anymore. Text, graphics, sound, and video are now part of our daily lives. The television we watch uses it. We carry mobile devices that incorporate it. Apps are filled with text, graphics, and sound. The visual world with text and sound is all around us. It is there to entertain, educate, and inform. Those who provide the content know how to use it to their advantage, including the movie, gaming, and advertising industries.

The movie industry has had a long history of providing stunning visuals. The tools at its disposal did not include the computer and processing power that we have today. Practical methods were used to create visual sights and sounds. Huge landscapes and jaw-dropping backdrops were created using canvases and paints. The effects, which still impress us today, were painstakingly built from scratch.

In the past twenty-five years, those visuals have gone from traditional canvas and paint to computer and mouse generated. Computers have made it easier to create those effects. Twenty years ago, the cost of such technology went beyond the budget of many libraries and museums. These specialized tools were only available to those in the industry who could afford them. In addition, the technology was massive to house and maintain. Servers that were used to process even the simplest of effects filled entire rooms. These effects, which are commonly referred to as computer-generated imagery (CGI), are what is used to create those stunning visuals today.

CGI effects are no longer limited to the movie industry giants. The average user can now create the same effects with a laptop computer. Such processing power is even possible in our mobile devices. The hardware has become so affordable that anyone with a few hundred dollars can be a part of this exciting field.

Additionally, software has become much easier to use, and these applications are no longer the tools of graphic artists and animation specialists alone. The cost for this software today is either free or low cost. Even the most powerful software is affordable for those who want to create exciting visuals.

The movie industry is not the only one pushing visuals and technology forward. The video gaming industry has been a strong and driving force in visuals. Gamers have always demanded the best graphics possible. It is this demand that often pushes new technology and graphic standards. This movement helps to develop tools and visuals that benefit digital exhibits. Much of what developers use to create software comes from the gaming industry.

Graphics are not the only advancement the gaming industry is pushing forward. Gamers have had a long desire to interact with games that go beyond the traditional hands-on controllers. The industry has recognized this and it has moved us beyond what we imagined to be possible twenty or thirty years ago. They have helped to introduce us to hand-free gaming as well as touch-and-voice–activated games.

One of the most important needs of gamers is accuracy and speed. And as such, gamers are the most critical when evaluating new controllers. The industry recognizes a high standard. This has led to the development of some of the most amazing devices. These devices do not just end up in the hands of gamers. They end up being used by the nongamer as well. The technology finds its way into places that one might not even consider, areas such as museums and libraries, where they can be used to enhance the experience of digital exhibits.

The advertising industry is another field that knows how to use these cutting-edge technologies in order to get their products out into the world. Advertisers understand the importance of the digital world. The tools that are used to create stunning visuals are well known to them. However, once again, these powerful tools are not exclusive to this industry. Much of what they use is easily obtainable by libraries to create and build extraordinary digital exhibits.

Librarians and museums want to be able to show off their digital collections. The need to share and educate users has always been prevalent in the mission of libraries and museums. Taking the same ideas and creativity from advertisers, as well as the film and video game industries, is a great way produce stunning digital exhibits.

Libraries and museums have incorporated digital exhibits for quite some time. Digital exhibits and collections go beyond simple digital displays. Visitors are being engaged with exhibits that reach more than just the visual senses. Sound and touch play a major role as well.

As technology has become more advanced, digital exhibits have incorporated many of these exciting new technologies. Those who develop and create have taken advantage of these new tools and incorporated the use of devices such as tablets and mobile smartphones into their projects. Content is no longer limited to local hosting, and actually much of today's digital collection is being stored in the cloud or offsite on private servers. This type of storage is making it not only easier to access but also easier to maintain. Preservation and archival software products such as Rosetta from Ex Libris are making it easier to maintain digital content. And that content is reaching a broader audience.

IMPORTANCE OF DIGITAL EXHIBITS

Librarians have always surrounded themselves with new and exciting technology. Libraries and museums continue to embrace technology through innovative digital exhibits. Visitors no longer have to experience exhibits that are only visual. Libraries and museums can bring patrons into a more immersive world through an exhibit that allows them to navigate through images and text by using natural motions, such as waving a hand to turn a page.

Information is no longer limited to the confines of the small virtual real estate. Bigger data storage is available and it is no longer limited by technology and cost. Digital exhibits will benefit greatly from this expanded space. Users will be able to access the added content directly from their mobile devices. Rare books and objects will find a new medium of digital representation. And all of this will help libraries (and their exhibits) reach a broader audience.

PROJECTS

The projects in this book range from using just software to using both hardware and software. Each project is detailed so any institution can implement it. The level of each project is designed so that any beginner can implement any project. More advanced users will be able to improve on the basics of the projects. Most projects use software that is completely free. Other projects require licenses to run the specific hardware. Much of the costs for hardware is far more inexpensive than one might expect. Technology such as Microsoft Kinect has become affordable for even some of the tightest budgets. That budgeted scope allows for some very exciting and useful digital exhibits.

Incorporating a digital exhibit is no longer a project for those with advanced skills in technology. It is not limited to those with budgets for highly expensive equipment and software. The movie, gaming, and advertising industries do not hold a monopoly on digital creativity. Hundreds of staff members are no longer needed to create even the more advanced digital exhibits.

With the advancement in technology and affordability, libraries and museums have the power to create stunning and exciting digital exhibits. The chapters in this book are designed to help you enter the world of digital exhibits and create your own. Those who find themselves hesitant to begin will find it easy with these simple projects. Soon you will find yourself comfortable with the digital exhibit world and will gain enough knowledge to go out and seek new tools and technologies.

2

GETTING STARTED WITH DIGITAL COLLECTIONS AND EXHIBITS

COPYRIGHT

Before getting started with a digital exhibit, you will want to ensure that all the proper permissions have been obtained. It is not enough to assume that if your collection has a printed copy of a work that it is fair to make a digital copy. The same is true for digital formats. Many publishers set a limit on what can and cannot be converted to other formats. For example, one of the projects in this book requires image formats. If the content that a publisher provides is an e-book, you may not have permission to extract or convert the entire content to image format. Ensure that you are aware of the publisher's copyright restrictions.

This book is intended to provide you with the tools and how-to instructions on creating a digital exhibit for display. Providing details of copyright laws goes beyond the scope of this book. Librarians are well aware of the importance of copyright law and know where to find the right resources on the subject. It is best to understand the copyright of the material you are using, because much of your digital exhibit could end up being online.

CONTENT

A digital exhibit and collection is only as good as its content. When choosing content, make sure that it is relevant to the type of exhibit you are going to create. Images should be of the highest quality. Many of the projects in this book use images. These images often have to be in very specific sizes. Some applications will either scale up or scale down an image. If your images are of a low resolution, scaling up will result in poor quality images that will look blurred. Make sure the images you obtain are of the highest resolution possible. If you are creating your own images by scanning print items, make sure to use a high resolution of 300 DPI (dots per inch) or more. This will yield the best results.

While working with your digital content, remember the importance of scalability. Your images might be of a high resolution, but that is not the same as image size. The actual size should be consistent with your digital project. For example, suppose you are to going to set up a large digital display that uses 1920-by-1080 screen resolution. This is the typical resolution for larger high-definition displays. Adding images with a size of 192-by-108 will not work well in that display. The reason is that the image will have to be scaled up to reach the 1920-by-1080 resolution, which will result in a blurred image. However, scaling down an image does not give the same negative effect.

Just as the resolution and size are important, the actual size in disk space is also important. Many of the digital cameras today use high-resolution images. They capture images that are sixteen megapixels or more, which results in images that are 4928-by-3264 in size. Such large dimensions can be scaled down within the application that runs the digital exhibit. But the actual size in memory might create longer load times. The digital exhibit might suffer from a slight lag time when switching between images. It is best not to exceed the dimensions of your project. Image resolution and size are key attributes in your content.

Providing appropriate descriptions is also important. They should be relevant, accurate, and easy to read. The content you use will not only come from images, but much of it will also consist of text, which may or may not accompany an image. Remember that users will be using a digital display of some kind to access your digital exhibit. If you are creating an online exhibit, then having lengthy descriptions that are detailed is fine. Users viewing the online exhibit will be accessing it in their own comfort and using a device with which they can take their time. On the other hand, if the digital exhibit is a large display kiosk, the users' attention is often limited. It is limited to the time they want to spend standing in front of the kiosk. In this instance, it is best to be precise and limit the amount of detail. Add content that is relevant and important. Any additional details that can be obtained by further reading are best kept out of the descriptions. The purpose of the digital exhibit is to inform and educate the users. Show them as much of your content as possible. If they want to know more, they can access additional information on their own.

Know your intended audience and try to be inclusive for all targeted audiences. Guidelines to the type of content will come from your institution. It is always best to get feedback for any content you may think is questionable. If possible, ask for feedback and input from targeted audiences when choosing content. What might work for some groups may not work for all groups. Including all audiences is not always possible, so the goal is to target as many groups as you can with your content. Although it is impossible to get the exact content correct, taking the time to understand your audience will benefit your digital exhibit greatly.

LOCATION

Location, location, location! That is not just something that holds true for realtors. In digital exhibits and collections, the same is true. This includes both physical space and virtual space. Unlike the real estate market, digital exhibits are often limited in the choice of location. Many exhibits are just given a space to work with and you are told to make it happen. Regardless of whether you are allowed to choose the right location or are given a space, location is always important.

Plan ahead by scoping out the possible locations for a digital exhibit. Survey each potential location, making a list of pros and cons. Not only should you keep in mind the type of digital exhibit you are going to install, but you should also be mindful of future digital exhibits that can be put in that location. The world of digital exhibits is constantly evolving. What might work great now in that location might be considered obsolete in the future. Perhaps a new and exciting technology could arise? Here is a list of some of the things that one should be looking for in a location:

- *Proper electrical power sources.* Outlets from above and below are ideal. Some projects will use projectors, so having ceiling-level power sources is a great way to conceal wires.
- *Adequate lighting.* Some exhibits benefit from a lot of light, while others might require low light. This is especially important if your digital exhibit will be part of a physical exhibit as well. Make sure the location is capable of changing the lighting from high to low. Check with your building maintenance department for any specifications.
- *Size of the location.* Make sure that any projectors, displays, or kiosks will fit properly. Checking that they fit in the location is not always enough. Some projects use projectors to project across long distances. If you are creating a large display, make sure the distance between the projector and the display is large enough.
- *Flow of traffic.* Some digital exhibits are often placed in areas where there is high traffic. Make sure there is plenty of space for users to experience your exhibit without impeding the flow of traffic. Your exhibit should be free of any potential bottlenecks.
- *Privacy and comfort.* If you are creating a digital exhibit that is interactive, consider the user's privacy and comfort. Don't choose a location that is going to make the user feel as if he or she were on display. If the intent of your digital exhibit is to showcase users, then privacy may not be important. For instance, imagine a digital exhibit that uses hands-free interaction to manipulate a screen. Your exhibit might have a second large display that allows others to view the person interacting with the display. In this case, privacy and comfort might not be an issue.

Consult with the museum or library director, staff, and/or faculty who are in charge of the space. Before starting your project, make sure that you have all the permissions to install and alter any location. It would be a shame if your exciting digital exhibit could not be put into place because of minor details.

As stated before, virtual location is just as important as physical location. Why is virtual location important? It is important because this is where visitors will find your online digital exhibit. If you are using a hosted site that does not offer your own domain name, this makes your online exhibit look unprofessional and unpolished. If they only offer a subdomain, visitors might be confused as to which site they are visiting. For example, suppose you use a hosting site called freewebsights.com. The hosting site might give you a subdomain for your exhibit, which you might call abclibraryexhibit. That subdomain would be abclibraryexhibit.freewebsights.com. Someone visiting your site might think that it is part of freewebsights.com. It is much preferable to have a subdomain that uses your institution's domain name, such as ourexhibit.abclibrary.org.

BUDGET

Budgeting is often tricky and difficult. Sometimes you will find your budget either coming up short or going over budget. If you are asked to propose a budget, it is best to allot for the best-quality hardware within reason. This does not mean you ask for the highest-priced items. It simply means you ask for hardware that has proven quality and can be used for a few years to come.

If you are given a fixed budget, as most librarians are, or if your budget is limited, then selection is limited and you must be a little creative. One area where you don't have to choose the most expensive equipment is computers. All of the projects in this book do not require a lot of processing power. Many digital exhibits can be run on a tablet that costs a few hundred dollars. That includes the computer, display, and input device to run a digital exhibit.

Displays are often tricky. Make sure to allow enough in your budget to obtain a high-quality display. The same will hold true for projectors. Other devices such as mounting hardware are also important. Do not budget for low-quality mounting hardware. Remember that the mounting hardware is going to support the more expensive display!

It is a best practice to try to distribute evenly for the project. Some costs may be higher than others, but make justifications for those higher costs based on quality and need. Electronic hardware might cost more than the materials that help create the exhibit, such as print mounting and furniture. Begin by budgeting enough for digital hardware. Even on a low budget, it is important to get the best-quality equipment for the digital exhibit.

PROJECT SELECTION

Carefully select the project that best fits your content, location, and budget. If you are just starting out and your skill set is very limited, to the point that you are not sure what to choose, choose a project that is smaller in scope. Start out with something that is easy to implement and does not require a lot of expensive hardware.

Chapter 5 lists several projects that range from online exhibits to hands-free exhibits. These projects are designed so that anyone can get them up and running. Some projects may appear to be advanced in nature. Do not let that discourage you from choosing them, especially if you have implemented digital exhibits in the past. For those who are advanced users, don't let the simplicity of these projects turn you away either. These projects were chosen so that advanced users can build upon them and make them even better! The great thing about digital exhibits is that they can always be improved on with more creativity. No matter what skill level you are at with working on digital exhibits, any project you choose will be worth implementing and possibly improving.

3

TOOLS AND APPLICATIONS

YOUR WEAPON OF CHOICE

This chapter is design to give you suggestions for tools to create stunning digital collection exhibits, the majority of which are either open source or free. You are not confined, however, to only using these free applications. Feel free to use others you are comfortable with or already own.

Below is a list of the tools and applications that will be useful for the upcoming projects in this book:

- GIMP 2
- Image Resizer for Windows
- Microsoft Expression Web 4
- Notepad
- Audacity
- Moovly
- Microsoft Research Image Composite Editor
- Microsoft Wireless Display Adapter
- Android, iPad, Windows 8 Tablet, and All-in-One

GIMP 2

GIMP 2 is a free image manipulation program. It is available at http://www.gimp.org/. Although it is not as robust as Adobe Photoshop, it does an excellent job at manipulating images and adding layers. There are several tools and filters that can be applied. The program allows for easy transformation, such as scaling and cropping. GIMP 2 supports several image formats, from JPG, GIF, TIFF, PNG, and many other special file formats. Imported images can be exported easily. GIMP 2 is a great tool for quickly manipulating images. The learning curve is not as steep as with other applications such as Photoshop. GIMP 2 is available for both Windows and Mac as well as Linux.

Image Resizer for Windows

Oftentimes using an application to resize an image like GIMP 2 can take some time to load and resize. Sometimes you just want to adjust the picture quickly. Rather than spending time looking for the application, opening up the file, and clicking through options to simply resize an image, it would be much easier if there was an option to right-click and resize the file on the fly. Unfortunately, Windows currently does not offer that feature as standard.

Luckily, there is a program that does just that, one simple right-click to resize an image. Image Resizer for Windows is available at https://imageresizer.codeplex.com/. This program will install the right-click feature that allows for image resizing without having to open a separate application.

Once installed, simply right-click on any image saved on the computer. It will launch a tiny application box that will resize the image. The tiny program is easy to use. Simply select the new image size:

- Small (854 × 480)
- Medium (1366 × 768)
- Large (1920 × 1080)
- Mobile (320 × 480)
- Custom

In addition to the size, there are three options:

- Only Shrink Pictures: Image will only scale down.
- Replace the Originals: New resized image will replace original.

- Ignore Picture Rotation: Automatic image rotation correction will not be used.

Microsoft Expression Web 4

Many librarians have grown accustomed to using Adobe Dreamweaver (DW). It seems to be the choice of many librarians. DW is an excellent tool for designing websites and working with web-based files. The problem is that DW is expensive, so some of the added features might not justify the cost and many librarians' limited budgets.

Microsoft Expression Web 4 (MEW4) is a free alternative to DW. Although there are many other free alternatives to DW, MEW4 has a lot of the same features as DW and its look and feel is similar to that of DW. Those who are familiar with DW will take to MEW4 with great ease. MEW4 has the capability to upload files to a remote server, just as DW does. This makes web development easier, rather than using a separate FTP client. MEW4 is available for free download at http://www.microsoft.com/en-us/download/details.aspx?id=36179.

Notepad

As Image Resizer for Windows is to GIMP, Notepad is to MEW4. Oftentimes files will have to be updated. The task might be to simply change one line in a file. Opening up MEW4 seems to be a bit too much. An easier approach would be to use a simple text editor. There are several other free text editors, such as Notepad++ or Textpad. Those editors have more tools than Notepad, which may seem useful. But the purpose of Notepad is to get in and out quickly. The other huge benefit to Notepad is that it comes loaded standard with every Windows machine. There is no need to install it. If you are borrowing a computer to make quick edits, Notepad is always available on the Windows machine you are using.

Notepad also allows you to open and save almost any text-based file. Such files that are common for digital exhibits are CML, XML, CSS, JS, HTML, and PHP. Notepad makes it easier to save those files to a new format. Simply add the file extension with double quotes. An example would be saving a PHP file, "myfile.php." Although Notepad is lacking in robust features compared to Notepad++, it is still very quick in making and saving changes to a file.

It is important to note that when choosing a text editor, whether it is Notepad or some other text editor, avoid using applications such as Microsoft Word or Wordpad. Those applications are designed for documents. Using them will alter the layout of the text file because they add formatting to the text.

Audacity

Although none of the projects in this book incorporate audio, it does not mean that audio cannot be used in digital exhibits. So including a program that is great for audio is important to add to your computer. Audacity is a simple yet powerful application that offers audio recording, playback, and editing. It is available for free at http://audacity.sourceforge.net/. It is available for Windows, Mac, and Linux. Audacity has the following features:

- Record live audio.
- Record computer playback on any Windows Vista or later machine.
- Convert tapes and records into digital recordings or CDs.
- Edit WAV, AIFF, FLAC, MP2, MP3, or Ogg Vorbis sound files.
- AC3, M4A/M4R (AAC), WMA, and other formats supported using optional libraries.
- Cut, copy, splice, or mix sounds together.
- Numerous effects including change in speed or pitch of a recording.

Moovly

Digital exhibits often incorporate video to help illustrate an exhibit. Presentation videos can be created by using a variety of commercial software such as Microsoft PowerPoint, Techsmith Camtasia, and Adobe Illustrator. Online presentation software such as Prezi is also popular. The trouble with many of these is oftentimes a combination of cost, learning curve, and scalability. For instance, Camtasia is excellent at making animated presentation videos, but the cost is often not suitable for some budgets (although they do offer educational pricing as well as a free thirty-day trial). Prezi is a great online tool, however, it is limited in scope.

Moovly is an online application that is free to low cost, easy to use, and scalable. Moovly's sign-up process at https://editor.moovly.com/en/register/free is simple; one can even sign up using a Facebook account. The free account is limited, but users are given plenty of features included in the free account that allow you to create professional-looking animated videos:

- Unlimited number of videos
- Ten-minute maximum video
- Standard definition 480P resolution
- One hundred MB/twenty items of storage (items include uploaded images and sound clips)
- Two standard Moovly item libraries
- Ability to upload images and sound clips
- YouTube and Facebook export

Upgraded accounts range from $9.95 to $24.95 per month (at the time of writing). Each upgrade level offers more features such as watermark removal, increased storage space, and video upload.

Moovly's interface is entirely online and web based. There is no stand-alone program that can be installed on a PC. All content is hosted online in the cloud. The interface is very similar to Camtasia and others, such as Cyberlink's PowerDirector. It uses a timeline where images, video, and sound clips are dragged and dropped into the timeline. Items can be from the standard Moovly library, which is completely searchable. Items can also be uploaded and used within the timeline.

The free account is limited to twenty uploaded items. This may seem like a limitation that can become frustrating. However, Moovly is unique in that once an item is inserted and saved to a project, the item is no longer needed, unless you want to reuse it. Moovly's technique of saving an item when saving a project is very practical. This is ideal compared to applications such as Apple's iMovie for the iPad, in which removing an item from the iPad also removes it from all iMovie projects.

One trick for allowing unlimited item usage in Moovly is to upload, insert, and delete the item from your library. The extra steps may seem tedious, but it allows you to use more items across several projects.

Microsoft Research Image Composite Editor

Of all the recommended applications in this chapter, Microsoft Research's Image Composite Editor (ICE) is the only one that will be needed for any of the projects in chapter 5. Therefore, it is recommended that it be downloaded and installed. ICE is available for free from Microsoft Research at http://research.microsoft.com/en-us/um/redmond/groups/ivm/ICE/.

Microsoft ICE is a powerful panoramic stitching editor. The application takes a series of overlapping images from a scene and stitches them together into one high-resolution image. The image created looks seamless and is great for use in digital exhibits. The panoramic image can be saved into various image formats. It can also be saved in multitiled format for high-definition viewers. Multitiled format allows for viewing and seamlessly rendering scenes. This is great for digital exhibits where users can pan and zoom across a large image. A perfect example would be a panoramic view of the Grand Canyon.

As noted, chapter 5 includes a project that will use a panoramic image for high-definition view. Here are instructions for how to create an HD View image. Begin by installing both ICE and the HD View. HD View is available for download at http://research.microsoft.com/en-us/um/redmond/groups/ivm/HDView/. Installation for each application is simple, just follow the prompts to install.

Start by taking a series of overlapping images with a digital camera. If your camera has a panoramic setting, do not use it. Begin at one end of the scene and take several images as you move slowly in the direction of the scene. Make sure the scene is relatively calm. Taking a series of shots at a sporting event, where players are moving around, is not recommended.

While taking the shots, be sure to keep the camera as level as possible. It is okay if the camera is not perfectly aligned, but obvious shifts in the camera's angle may yield poor results. When taking the overlapping pictures, make sure that the images overlap. You do not have to make every shot perfectly aligned with the previous shot. ICE will do the work of seamlessly stitching the scene together. This makes it not only easier to create a scene, but also less stressful to take the images.

Once all the images have been taken, upload them to the computer and open up the ICE program (figure 3.1).

Insert the images taken by either going to **File > New Panorama...** or by dragging all the selected images onto the gray area. Make sure to select all the images at once. Once the images are added, ICE will begin stitching them together automatically. If the images are not overlapping, ICE will return an error.

Next select the type of export. For the purposes of this book, select **Deep Zoom Tileset.** Click on **Deep Zoom settings...** and make sure the *viewer* is set to **Automatic**. Also make sure the *size* is set to **Entire web page**. Click **Export to disk...** and save it in a separate folder. ICE will generate the panoramic image and create a folder with the name entered as well as four files with the name you have chosen.

- *mypano_stitch_hdv.xml*
- *mypano_stitch.html*
- *mypano_stitch.xml*
- *HDViewSL.xap*

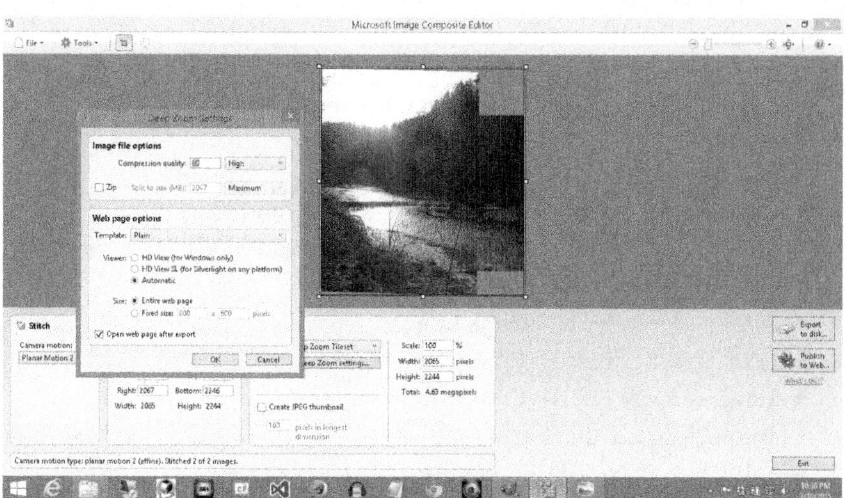

Figure 3.1. Microsoft Image Composite Editor

After the files are created, ICE will launch the default browser on the system and display the panoramic image. The image may also be opened by clicking the HTML file that was created above. Once loaded in the browser, make sure the image is correct and you are satisfied with the results. If the desired view in not acceptable, try taking the images again.

ICE is an excellent and easy-to-use application for creating panoramic images for high-definition viewing. It is great for creating backdrop images that can be used within a digital exhibit's webpage. They can also be used for more advanced digital exhibits for panning and zooming, such as one of the projects in chapter 5.

Microsoft Wireless Display Adapter

Digital exhibits should be designed and implemented as cleanly as possible with minimal visual impact from hardware. One of the biggest distractions you can have at your digital exhibit is an unsightly tangle of cables. Power cables for displays or projectors can often be hidden behind the display, but display cables are often harder to disguise or hide.

Intel developed Wireless Display (WiDi), which uses the Miracast standard protocol to allow a connection over WiFi to an external display. Its design allows the computer to wirelessly project output to an external display, and there is no need for a video output cable. In order to take advantage of Intel's WiDi, your computer must have the following common specifications. The processor must be one of the following:

- 2nd generation Intel Core i3/i5/i7 Mobile Processor
- 3rd Generation Intel Core i3/i5/i7 Mobile and Desktop Processor
- 4th Generation Intel Core i3/i5/i7 Mobile and Desktop Processor
- Intel Pentium N3510 Processor
- Intel Celeron N2805 Processor
- Intel Celeron N2810 Processor
- Intel Celeron N2910 Processor
- Intel Atom Z3740 Processor
- Intel Atom Z3740D Processor
- Intel Atom Z3770 Processor
- Intel Atom Z3770D Processor

The graphics must have one of the following:

- Intel Iris Pro Graphics 5200
- Intel Iris Graphics 5100
- Intel HD Graphics 5000
- Intel HD Graphics 4600
- Intel HD Graphics 4400
- Intel HD Graphics 4200
- Intel HD Graphics 4000
- Intel HD Graphics 3000 (mobile)
- Intel HD Graphics 2500
- Intel HD Graphics 2000 (mobile)

The WiFi adapter must have one of the following:

- Intel Centrino Wireless-N 1000, 1030, 2200, or 2230
- Intel Centrino Wireless-N 2200 for Desktop
- Intel Centrino Advanced-N 6200, 6205, 6230, or 6235
- Intel Centrino Advanced-N 6205 for Desktop
- Intel Centrino Wireless-N + WiMAX 6150
- Intel Centrino Advanced-N + WiMAX 6250
- Intel Centrino Ultimate-N 6300
- Intel Dual Band Wireless-N 7260
- Intel Dual Band Wireless-AC 7260
- Intel Dual Band Wireless-AC 7260 for Desktop
- Intel Dual Band Wireless-AC 3160
- Intel Wireless-N 7260
- Broadcom BCM43228
- Broadcom BCM43241
- Broadcom BCM4352

The operating system must be one of the following:

- Windows 7
- Windows 8
- Windows 8.1

Fortunately, most of the Windows tablets, laptops, and all-in-one PCs that have been released in recent years meet all of these requirements.

Along with a WiDi enabled computer, a wireless adapter will be needed. Microsoft offers a WiDi wireless adapter that retails for $59.95 (at the time of writing). The adapter takes advantage of true Miracast technology. The device is easy to install and set up; connecting to the device takes only a few seconds.

Microsoft's device differs from other wireless display technologies. It offers true one-to-one mirror casting. Mirror casting is the ability to display the entire desktop or extended desktop to an external display. This allow for true streaming of virtually all media content. Other devices offer limited casting, which only displays certain media using apps.

The Microsoft Miracast device allows for displaying duplicate or an extended desktop. This type of wireless mirroring is an excellent way to rid a digital exhibit display of unwanted visible wires. Now a display can be mounted in one area and the computer can be housed in a nearby area. This is also great for maintenance and security. Because the computer is placed away from the display, access and security are easier. You do not have to be creative in trying to disguise the wires and computer for the exhibit.

The WiDi technology uses one other important technology, which is WiFi. The wireless device needs to be broadcasting and discoverable over a WiFi network. Larger WiFi networks will often have a harder time discovering the device to pair with the computer. This can be due to ports being closed by the network administrator or the heavy traffic that exists on the WiFi network. It is best to consult with your network administer before using a wireless display device over your institution's WiFi network.

If connection to the device is not possible due to the conditions listed above, there is an alternative option to get the devices to pair together. You could use a wireless router to broadcast a non-Internet enabled WiFi network. An inexpensive router can be purchased for less than $50. Your network administrator may even have a spare router that can be used. Power the WiFi router and make sure the device is broadcasting, so that the wireless display adapter can discover it and the computer with WiFi can connect to the private wireless network. Make sure that the router is secured with an encryption key in order to prevent users from trying to connect and change your settings. Your network administrator can help you with setting up everything. If your digital exhibit's content needs Internet access, you will need to check with your network administrator to see if you are allowed to enable Internet for your WiFi router. Some network administrators do not allow an external WiFi router to access and compete with existing wireless networks for their institution.

Android Devices

Digital exhibits have benefited greatly from the invention of mobile tablets. Exhibits can take advantage of these precise touch devices. Their precision is much more accurate than the touchscreens of the past. The cost of implementing a touch kiosk is inexpensive compared to traditional touch display kiosks, which consisted of both a touchscreen and computer to run. Their cost could be three to four times the cost of an average tablet.

Android tablets and hand-held devices are the least expensive option for mobile kiosks. Many devices running the latest flavor of Android can be purchased for under $100 (at the time of writing). Because the devices are designed for low power consumption, powering them is ideal for kiosks that run all day.

Low power consumption is not the only benefit of Android devices when it comes to digital exhibits. Android devices also come in a wide range of display sizes, ranging from small five-inch screens to ten-inch screens. The devices also come in different processor and graphics configurations. Android's memory is also upgradable. This can be very useful when running kiosks that require all of its content to be installed on the mobile device.

One drawback is that the Android device is limited to running apps from the App Store, and many of these apps are not specifically designed for digital exhibits. Although custom apps can be run without going through the App Store, this approach is often difficult because it requires having your own developers create a custom app. Such resources are not often available in a library or museum. The amount of money and resources may prove to be unjustifiable.

The Android device is capable of mirror casting. The setup is not difficult, but depending on the Android device, it can be different from device to device. Another drawback to Android mirroring is that it only mirrors the display on the tablet. This may seem useful when displaying the content on a larger screen, but for digital exhibits, it is not ideal. An ideal setup would consist of the display being extended. This would allow a kiosk front end on the tablet and digital content display on a larger extended screen.

One other drawback of the Android device is the lack of a native kiosk mode. There are several kiosk apps in the App Store, but those apps have limitations and often require updates. The native kiosk mode for tablets is very important for digital exhibits. It allows the exhibit to run a single app that users cannot shut down to run another app.

Because Android tablets come in different sizes, finding a matching kiosk stand can be a challenge. Companies such as Maclocks offer kiosk solutions for Android devices, but it is not possible for them to include all the different devices that are on the market. If you are using an Android device, it is best to make sure that a kiosk stand is available for the device you intend to use.

Apple iPads

The Apple iPad seems to be the preferred choice for touchscreen kiosks in digital exhibits. Just like the Android, the iPad has similar benefits. One benefit of using the iPads for kiosks is its solid operating system. Apple's iOS is easy to use and its apps are stable. Another appeal is that the iPad is the only device that runs Apple's iOS, unlike the Android device that can be run from several manufactures from Samsung to Asus. Additionally, the iPad does not have many variations; the iPad, iPad Air, and iPad Mini are the currently available models, which vary in memory, size, and price. Therefore, finding a kiosk enclosure is much easier because the iPad size is the same for each model.

Although the iPad has these advantages over the Android when looking for a kiosk tablet, the iPad does have its own limitations. The biggest issue is the lack of memory upgrade, even with the model that offers the highest memory; 128 gigabytes of storage seems as if it would be more than enough, but given the size of content that can be used in a digital exhibit, 128 GB will fill up rather quickly. If you are on a budget, purchasing the lower sixteen GB model may prove to be a poor decision in the future because it is not upgradable like other tablets on the market.

Apple has also been known to drop support for their iPad products rather quickly. The first-generation iPad was introduced in 2010. Apple dropped iOS support for the first-generation iPad in 2012, less than two years after it was introduced, although it still had much use for digital exhibits. Apple's drop in support is something to keep in mind when considering the iPad. Although technology changes rather quickly, two years is a short time for a device to lose support, especially when the device is coming from an industry giant whose product is still viable.

Apple's iPad also costs more compared to an Android device. The sixteen GB iPad Air 2 retails for $499 and the 128 GB model retails for $699, compared to the Android Nexus 9 tablet, which retails for $399 (at the time of writing). Such a high price tag may not be justified for a kiosk; it all depends on the type of digital exhibit that will be implemented.

Like the Android device, the iPad is limited to running apps from the Apple Store. Creating and running a custom app may be too costly, just as for the Android custom app. Where the Android device lacks kiosk mode, the iPad has done an excellent job at adding kiosk mode to their iOS. Enabling kiosk mode is easy and it allows you to control one app to run in kiosk mode. It also gives you the option to control which buttons the user can access for the touch and motion gestures. Such gestures include swipes to access iPad controls or motions that change the screen orientation. Kiosk mode also allows you to control which areas a user can access on the screen. This is very useful when running a web browser for which you want to restrict user access to the address bar, where you may want to have that area untouchable and inactive. To enter the iPad in kiosk mode:

- Open Settings
- Go to **General > Accessibility**
- Tap on Guided Access (Scroll down the page a little, it's under the "Learning" section)
- Flip the switch to ON
- Tap on Set Passcode (this will prevent users from leaving "Guided Access" mode)
- Enter a passcode

Next, open the app you wish to use in kiosk mode. Once the app is loaded, keep it running and enter "Guided Access." Click on the Home button three times. This will enter "Guided Access" with three options: Hardware Buttons, Touch, and Time Limit.

Hardware buttons allow you to enable or disable the sleep/wake button and volume buttons. It also allows you to enable or disable access to the keyboard and motions, such as rotating the screen by tilting the iPad. This type of control is great for instances where you may want to restrict access to some buttons but not all buttons. Perhaps you have an exhibit that uses sound. You might want to have the volume adjustable. At the same time you do not want the user to put the iPad in sleep mode. Because many kiosk enclosures do not block physical access to this button, this is an excellent option.

The touch option allows for partial or full restriction to screen. This option proves useful when running a slideshow of images that automatically rotate. Partial restriction is great for apps that have areas you don't want the user to access, but cannot turn off within the app itself. An example of this would be a simple gallery viewer that allows users to swipe left or right to view other images. The app might have buttons that allow the user access to options within the app. Disabling that area of the iPad is an easy way to turn off that option. To disable certain areas of the iPad, first slide the Touch Option to On. Next circle the areas where you do not want access on the iPad. The areas that are not touchable will be represented by a light gray circled area on the iPad. Make sure that the shadow effect does not distract users from the digital exhibit. Some may find that gray overlay unappealing.

Finally, guided access allows for time limits on the iPad. This option might be the least useful of the three. Setting a time limit might be a great idea for certain digital displays. The problem is that the time is not designed as one might think. Some might think that when the iPad times out, it restarts the app. That type of function would be ideal. Instead, it disables access to the iPad and requires a passcode to unlock and turn off guided access.

Microsoft Tablets

In 2012, Microsoft released their latest operating system called Windows 8. This version is a dramatic change from their previous operating systems as it is designed for mobile tablets as well as traditional desktops. This new operating system incorporates a new user experience and interaction that is similar to the Android and iOS, and users are given the same kind of functionality as other operating systems on the market. Windows 8 users are treated to a system that functions as a mobile device with the power of a fully functional PC. This break from the norm is great for digital exhibits.

Windows 8 also has faster boot times and can run using low power consumption. This type of power in such a small device is an excellent addition to the digital exhibits arsenal. Specially designed apps, as well as many offered in the App Store, run faster. They are designed to run intuitively, much like the apps that run on Android and iOS systems.

This new operating system has helped Microsoft enter the mobile device market. Manufacturers such as Hewlett-Packard, Dell, Asus, Lenovo, and others offer a wide range of devices that include tablets, two-in-one laptops, and all-in-one PCs that all run Microsoft Windows 8. Microsoft has even launched their own line of tablets: Surface Pro, Surface Pro 2, and Surface Pro 3.

Windows 8 does an excellent job at incorporating touch into their operating system. The operating system is not limited to apps from the App Store, and it can run traditional applications as well. Even powerful applications such as Microsoft Office run with ease on tablets. Custom applications and exhibits software will run as intended.

With such a wide variety of mobile devices, Windows 8 devices are ideal for digital exhibits, unlike iPads that are limited in size. Windows 8 devices that are touchscreen enabled come in tablet size to desktop screen size. A full-size all-in-one computer can be purchased for less than $1,000 (at the time of writing) with a twenty-inch or more screen size. These PCs are designed with mountable backs, which makes them ideal for kiosks mounted to walls or poles. For smaller tablets, the price is as low as a few hundred dollars. Such a low price fits even the tightest budgets.

Like iPads, Windows 8 devices offer kiosk mode. Microsoft recognized the value of using these devices as kiosks so they even made it easy to enable kiosk mode. Windows 8.1, the latest version, instructions are as follows:

- Log on to the device with an administrator account.
- Open PC Settings, click on Accounts, and create a new local user account by name.

- Log off the administrator account.
- Log in using the new local account that was created. This will install defaults for the local user.
- Log off the local account. Windows creates the profile for the local user.
- Once logged off the local account, log back in with an administrator account.
- Click on Set Up an Account for Assigned Access.
- Click on Choose an Account and then select the local.
- Once the local account is selected, click on the Choose an App button to assign the application the local user will use.
- Choose an app to assign.
- The selected application will launch for the local user the next time the local user account is logged in.

4

LIBRARY EXAMPLES AND CASE STUDIES

So now you have some background on digital exhibits, information on how to get started, and tools to work on creating an exciting exhibit. One of the best ways to gain inspiration for your exhibit is to look at what others are doing with their digital collections. This will help you to understand what pitfalls to avoid as well as learn about some interesting exhibits. The success of these libraries will inspire you to create a great exhibit. Let's take a look at some various case studies from different institutions.

REPURPOSED LAPTOPS PROJECT

Tarrant County College Northeast Campus Library | Ayyoub Ajmi, Library Technology Manager

Ayyoub Ajmi is a digital communications and learning initiatives librarian at University of Missouri–Kansas City (UMKC) School of Law. Before moving to the UMKC School of Law, Ayyoub was the library technology manager at the J. Ardis Bell Library of Tarrant County College (TCC) Northeast Campus. TCC has a total of five campuses that are located in Fort Worth, Arlington, and Hurst. Its fall 2014 student enrollment was about 50,628 students with a twenty-six-to-one student-to-faculty ratio (http://www.tccd.edu/about_tcc/quick_facts.html). Ayyoub was responsible for maintaining 120 desktop computers, thirty laptops, and many tablets. He was also responsible for the library's own network and various shared drives.

Ayyoub's inspiration for repurposing laptops for digital use began with his curiosity concerning one closet, which was located on the lower floor of the library's Computer Learning Center (CLC) but had no available key. Ayyoub decided to locate a key and discover what was stored in the closet. Upon opening it, he discovered thirty old laptops that had been stored there for years and forgotten. Typically, equipment is either disposed of or repurposed. These laptops were locked away and collecting dust.

Ayyoub decided to inspect the old laptops. Even though the laptops were collecting dust, they were still in working order. Because they were old, they did take some time to start up. He quickly learned that they were too old to repurpose for staff. This was due to the fact that they were too slow to run much of the applications that faculty and staff used in the library. The most important reason he could not reuse the laptops for staff is that they were running Windows XP, which was no longer supported at TCC.

So Ayyoub starting thinking of a way to reuse the laptops. One idea was to use them as loaner laptops for students. But like staff, students would not be satisfied using outdated laptops. In addition, Windows XP was no longer being supported on campus. By the end of the semester, Ayyoub learned at a staff meeting that the patron count was low. The director decided to be creative to increase it.

One of the initiatives to get patrons back into the library was to renovate with new furniture. This gave Ayyoub the idea of repurposing the laptops as digital displays. He also realized that some could be used as digital signage. Ayyoub began working with a team that included Bonnie Hodges, a public service librarian who still works at TCC; Amy Adams, a library manager who is no longer at TCC; and Ronald Ash, a library technician who passed away in December 2014.

Ayyoub and Ronald began working on a prototype. Ayyoub was aware that turning laptops into digital frames is not a new concept. He drew inspiration from a website by Werner Heuser (http://repair4laptop.org/notebook_picture_frame.html). In order to streamline and lighten the size and weight of the frames, they decided to strip them to the barest components possible. This included just the motherboard, LCD display, hard drive, and power source. Simple inexpensive wooden frames from the local craft store were used to enclose the digital components. Ayyoub joked by saying the cost was even less expensive because the frames were 50 percent off the day they purchased them.

After creating a prototype, the team decided to apply for a Title III grant to cover the costs and validate the project. At first they were rejected. This was partly due to the fact that those evaluating the grant application did not fully understand the project. The team reapplied for the grant and was awarded $1,500.

Once the grant was awarded, the team quickly began converting the rest of the old laptops. The conversion of all thirty laptops took about two months. The repurposed digital frames still ran Windows XP. Because the laptops did not need any access to the Internet, using the unsupported operating system was perfectly acceptable. This also helped to reduce the cost because there was no need to upgrade to Windows 7 or higher. The team also decided that the built-in image gallery screen saver was efficient enough to run the digital slide show on each frame. This also was a zero cost. The system's BIOS (basic input/output settings) were configured to ensure security and were programmed to turn displays on and off as needed. Finally, the USB ports were exposed so staff could easily update the frames with fresh content as needed.

Once all the laptops were converted to digital frames, they were ready to install. Mounting them to the walls was not difficult and took about two months. The biggest challenge for the team was making sure the electrical power was compliant and up to code. In most instances, power strips were used to power the frames. The team needed to make sure that none of the strips were overloaded or of low quality. Much of the cost for the exhibit consisted of power strips. The team spent a total of about $900 of the $1,500 from the grant.

Currently, the digital frames are located in both the main floor and the lower level of the library (figure 4.1). Each frame is based on the Dell Latitude PP01L laptops with a Pentium III and 256 MB of memory. Content displayed on the frames consists of digital photographs, digitized paintings, text, video and sound recordings, poems, and narration (http://libguides.tccd.edu/c.php?g=186471&p=1232254). Students, faculty, staff, and members of the community provide content via a participation request form.

When interviewing Ayyoub Ajmi, I asked him how come he didn't just dispose of the laptops from the beginning. He told me that as someone who came from Morocco in 2007, "Seeing thirty laptops that cost about $1,000, I didn't understand, because where I come from everything gets recycled." Ayyoub's understanding to recycle laptops along with his team's creativity designed a stunning digital exhibit that would fit just about any library budget.

Figure 4.1. Repurposed Laptop Project: Home. ***Image courtesy of Ayyoub Ajmi***

EXHIBIT SNAPSHOT

Houston Public Library | Roland Lemonius, Digital Projects Manager, HALAN Web Designer

Roland Lemonius is the digital projects manager and Houston Area Library Automated Network (HALAN) web designer for the Houston Public Library (HPL) at the Jesse H. Jones Building of the Central Library. Roland is responsible for working with the library's digital archives. He coordinates digital exhibits for the library. HPL holds 3.6

million items, and in 2014 it served 7.2 million in-person and online visitors (http://houstonlibrary.org/about-hpl). Roland also works as a web designer for the HALAN, which is responsible for five public libraries and one community college library in the Houston area. Roland has twenty years of experience in libraries.

The exhibit "Faces, Places & Spaces," which was on display at the HPL Julia Ideson Building from June 9, 2012, to September 1, 2012, is a collection of photographs of Houston residents from the 1880s to the 1920s. Images were captured by glass plate negatives. This type of photography is quite rare because advances in film photography have made plate negatives obsolete. The exhibit presents dozens of plates and photos that came from the collection at the Houston Metropolitan Research Center. The display allowed visitors to see the photography plates up close.

Because the exhibit ran for only a limited time, Roland wanted to "preserve" the experience of the physical exhibit in an online experience. Many physical exhibits just display their collection online. Roland wanted to capture the visiting experience of the exhibit for those who either couldn't or didn't have a chance to visit. Creating this type of online exhibit is also a great way to encourage visitors to come and see the exhibits at the library.

Exhibit Snapshot is unique in that it uses a panoramic tour of the library exhibit (figure 4.2). Online visitors are able to click on areas within the panoramic image. The user is given a clickable matrix of images. When they click on an individual image, a high-definition image is displayed along with metadata. Users can pan and zoom to see stunning details. Linking the images to the archives' website gives a better experience than just linking to a higher definition image. This connection to the library's digital archive also helps to promote and encourage the user to explore the library's digital archives.

To achieve the panoramic experience online, Roland, along with another team member, needed to take precise snapshots of the exhibit. Snapshots were taken in small increments, which was painstakingly slow. Fortunately, the exhibit was not too large. Another challenge for Roland's team was lighting. The library's natural lighting from above could change due to the weather. They had to ensure that the lighting was even. If it was not, then creating the panoramic image would be even more difficult and time consuming. Adobe Photoshop was used to

Figure 4.2. Exhibit Snapshot—Houston Public Library. ***Website capture. Digital Image. HMRC—Exhibit Snapshot. http://digital.houstonlibrary.org/virtual/faces-places***

create and edit the image. Photoshop was chosen due to its reputation in imaging software and Roland's experience in using it.

Many online 360-degree image tours in websites either use Adobe Flash or some other software that requires a plug-in that needs to be installed for each browser. Roland decided to use jQuery, which is a cross-platform JavaScript library. jQuery is unique in that it does not require separate plug-ins or other required files to work. Modern browsers support jQuery with ease. This means that a visitor accessing the Exhibit Snapshot does not have to install anything to make the 360-degree tour work. Roland's choice was also free to use. The jQuery plug-in can be obtained at http://likov.spb.ru/jquery-panorama-plugin/. HTML5 was also used in the design of the website.

HPL's Exhibit Snapshot is a great example of how a physical exhibit can be preserved as an online exhibit. It not only promotes the digital collection but it also encourages patrons to visit the physical library. Visitors will find themselves wanting to know more. The choice to use straight HTML5 and jQuery is also an added benefit to users because there are no unnecessary plug-ins to download and install.

THE VISIBLE STORAGE TABLET TOUR

Binghamton University | Kate Ellenberger, PhD Archaeology Student

The Art Museum at Binghamton University features several exhibits with works ranging from art drawings to approximately 3,000 permanent collected objects and many objects on loan. The museum exhibits are installed in the Main Gallery, the Susan M. Reifer '65 and Stanley J. Reifer '64 Mezzanine Gallery, and the Nancy J. Powell Gallery. The Main Gallery also has many smaller galleries. The director of the Art Museum is Diane Butler, PhD.

In the lower level galleries, the museum has a study room where visitors can engage with art. The Kenneth C. Lindsay Study Room allows students, faculty, and the general public to interact with any work in the permanent collection. Recently, the area installed glass cabinets in which objects that remain in storage can now be viewed by visitors. The objects are densely installed in the cabinets.

Because the objects in the glass cabinets are very close to one another, labeling each item would become an issue. The museum wanted to have a system that would allow visitors to not only see the works of art, but also read more information about an object. They also needed a way to "virtually" label each item, so that visitors would know more about it.

Kate Ellenberger is a PhD archaeology student at Binghamton University whose interests include community-based archaeology, and she developed the Visible Storage Tablet Tour. The system consists of a digitally organized collection that is stored in a database. Visitors use an Apple iPad to experience the tour. Two iPads are available for visitors to borrow as they view the glass cabinets. The cabinets include various objects from different time periods and regions around the world.

The tour is uniquely designed. Rather than labeling individual objects with a name, number, or code, visitors simply select a region on the iPad's graphical interface and then select an object. Items are grouped in separate regions. An overall image of the region is taken and inserted into the iPad. A user selects a specific object on the iPad within the overall region chosen. After clicking on the objects image, information is displayed about the selected object.

In addition to making basic information available, the system creates an interesting experience for visitors. Additional interaction allows them to choose brief labels about the object they are interested in. The labels are written by various students from different disciplines. The descriptions are not limited to those who installed the objects nor are they limited to art historians or members of the art community. A visitor can get a description from a comparative literature student or perhaps from an engineering student. This type of broad information gives the visitor a much more interesting and enjoyable experience.

In addition to the unique way of labeling the objects, Kate has also managed to implement a database system that is small in scope, but very practical and functional. The system resides entirely on the iPads. There is no need for an external server running a database. The iPad does not have to make any connections to an external source. This is important because the museum does not have a dedicated information technology department. A self-contained system is much easier to maintain. It also lowers the cost of having to purchase expensive servers and database software to run the system.

The system uses Filemaker Pro, which is a relational database from Filemaker Inc. The cross-platform is available for Apple systems. The database engine uses a graphical user interface to modify the database. Kate chose Filemaker Pro because of its ability to add elements. Unlike other database engines that require more work, Filemaker Pro is also beneficial because an iPad app is available for it. Filemaker Go, which is the mobile app for the iPad, has a kiosk mode. This feature was ideal for this project. Because the users would be walking around with an iPad, the system needed to be locked so visitors would not be able to access other functions on the iPad.

The database is also contained within a file that lives on each iPad. This level of security was important to the museum. They wanted to ensure that the information was only available to visitors when taking a tour. They did not want it published online or to allow users to have access outside the museum.

Kate, along with others from the Art Museum, have created an interesting exhibit. It is a low-cost solution to adding labels to objects that are densely organized in a cabinet. The addition of descriptions written from a student's perspective makes for an interesting and enjoyable experience. What is also worth noting for those who are thinking of adding a digital exhibit is that Kate's field of study is not in technology. Although Kate is technically savvy and has experience working in museums, her minimal solution yielded excellent results for such a small exhibit. Others in the information technology field might have approached the project with a much larger scope, thus making the project harder to manage and support.

STUDENT-CURATED EXHIBIT ON AFRICAN ART ALONG WITH THE AR MAGIC BOOK

Binghamton University Art Museum and University Libraries | Dr. Pamela Smart, Associate Professor Art History/ Anthropology; Benjamin Andrus, Reference/Subject Librarian; Mien Wong, Preservation Technician

The Binghamton University Art Museum continued its push for exciting exhibits by including innovative technology. The exhibition "Living Objects: Makers, Markets, Museum" is a collection of several African art objects. This exhibit also uses an exciting new invention that was developed at the Binghamton University Libraries called the AR Magic Book.

The exhibit is a collaboration of Pamela Smart and her thirty-six university students. The students are members of the "Museums and the Art of Exhibitions" and Anthropology/Art History course taught by Pamela at Binghamton University. A total of seventeen pieces of twentieth-century art from West Africa are on display in the lower galleries of the Art Museum. The pieces are on loan from a private collection of Michael Horowitz, a retired Binghamton University professor of anthropology, and his wife, Sylvia Horowitz.

The objects are from several different West African cultures: Baule, Dan, Dogon, Bambara, Igbo, Senufo, and Yoruba. The art was purchased during 1974–1975 when Horowitz and his family lived in Abidjan, the economic capital of Côte d'Ivoire. Horowitz recorded his acquisitions in great detail with journal entries; everything from the source, dimensions, location of purchase, and dealer's names.

The exhibition organizers wanted to not only showcase the pieces of art, but they also wanted to display Horowitz's journal. Unfortunately, the journal could not be put on display for fear that it might get damaged while on display.

Pamela had heard of an exciting new project that was being developed within the libraries at Binghamton University. She reached out to the project team, which consisted of the inventors, a library information technology specialist, a librarian, and a preservation specialist. The team demonstrated the AR Magic Book for Pamela and her anthropology/art history class.

The students were excited to see this new technology. They were also amazed that the library was developing such an exciting project. They immediately saw the potential for using the AR Magic Book in the exhibit (figure 4.3).

The AR Magic Book is designed to incorporate physical integration with digital presentation. This invention's goal is to bring back the natural feeling of viewing a book with the power of digital display.

The system consists of the following:

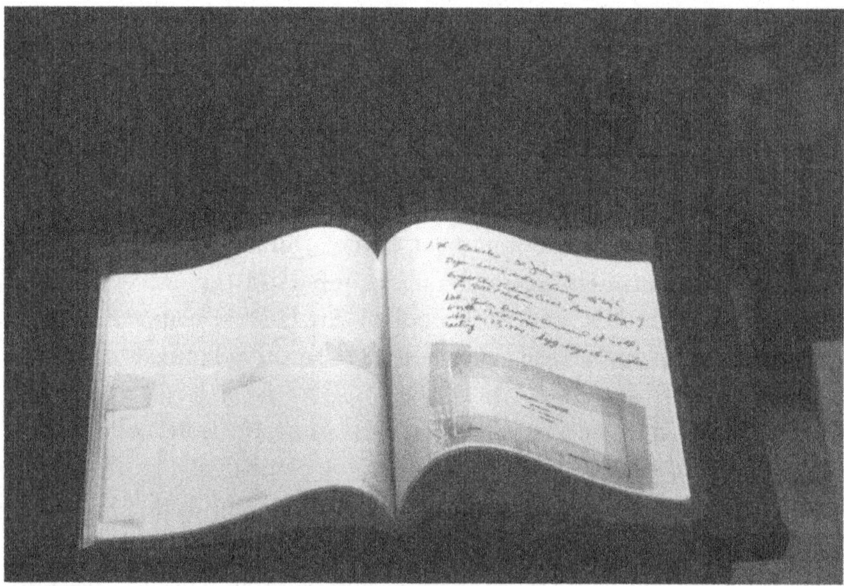

Figure 4.3. AR Magic Book. ***Digital Image. The AR Magic Book. Binghamton University Libraries. http://library2.binghamton.edu/news/ARMB***

- Blank viewing book with tiny glyphs printed on them
- Projector
- Camera

- Computer

Each component is combined to create a virtual viewing of Horowitz's journal. Visitors can interact with the journal as if it were an actual book on display. Content is typically displayed on a flat display, and users navigate using either a keyboard, mouse, or touchscreen. The AR Magic Book is different and gives the user a true natural interface.

Users turn each page as if they were using a regular book. There is no swiping of the hands or clicking on a mouse. Users can skip ahead, or move to the beginning, back, or middle. The system is designed to display each page as if it were a page in a printed book.

The system achieves this by reading tiny codes called glyphs. Each glyph is read by a camera. The corresponding page is displayed onto the blank book. The system is designed to have minimal load times between pages and to avoid any blanked-out effects while using the system. The goal is to create a visual effect and experience that is close to reading a physical book.

Setup for the AR Magic Book proved to be a challenge for the team. Because Pamela had only heard of the project a few weeks prior to the exhibition opening, the team had only a short time to install the AR Magic Book.

The AR Magic Book was still in development at the time of writing this book. The inventors began the project in late June 2014, and the exhibit debuted in mid-December 2014. Although several prototypes were created for the device's usage, none of them were designed for display in an art museum. The exhibit needed to have a setup that complemented Horowitz's collection and journal. It was important to avoid having the AR Magic Book overshadow everything else. They wanted to have the AR Magic Book displayed without the obvious intrusiveness, and they needed visitors to come across the display and be amazed by the technology while enjoying the journal.

To achieve this effect, the system was placed in a corner of the exhibit room. The lecture was installed on a wall. The book was displayed at a forty-five-degree angle, which made it challenging. The projector need to be mounted so that visitors would not find it obstructive.

Another challenge for the team was to minimize the number of wires coming from the projector and computer. The team decided to use wireless technology to send the display signal from the computer to the projector. Microsoft Miracast was used along with a WiDi-compatible laptop. This allowed for the laptop to sit at the gallery desk. The projector still required power, which could not be avoided. If the team had had more time, they would have drawn power from above the projector. The camera also needed to be connected to the laptop via a USB port. Again, avoiding the wire was not possible, so the team snaked the wire down the wall along the seams and cleverly masked the cable.

When the final installation was complete, the museum was pleased with the results. Those who attended the opening enjoyed the AR Magic Book. Despite the short amount of time, the installation ended up being minimal and looked professional.

5

STEP-BY-STEP LIBRARY PROJECTS FOR DIGITAL COLLECTIONS AND EXHIBITS

CREATE A DIGITAL EXHIBIT USING OMEKA

Omeka is a free open-source content management system for digital collections. It was developed by Roy Rosenzweig at the Center for History and New Media at George Mason University. This content management system (CMS) allows users to publish and exhibit digital content. Unique themes and plug-ins add much more functionality. Omeka uses an online dashboard and it allows users to easily search and manage content. Managing themes and plug-ins is also done on the dashboard. The dashboard is as simple to use as Wordpress's dashboard.

Now that you have a brief background on what Omeka is all about, this first project is going to show you how you can create a stunning digital exhibit using Omeka. For those of you who might be worried about setting up an Omeka site because you may think it involves a lot of technical details and configurations, do not worry; this project is the easiest of all the projects in this chapter. Once you are done setting up your own Omeka site, you will feel so empowered you will want to create even more exhibits (figure 5.1).

Omeka is a hosted service that offers both free and paid accounts. It is a great way for those who want to get started for free. The free account offers 500 MB of storage, one site, thirteen plug-ins, and five themes. Your site will have the latest version of Omeka with all the

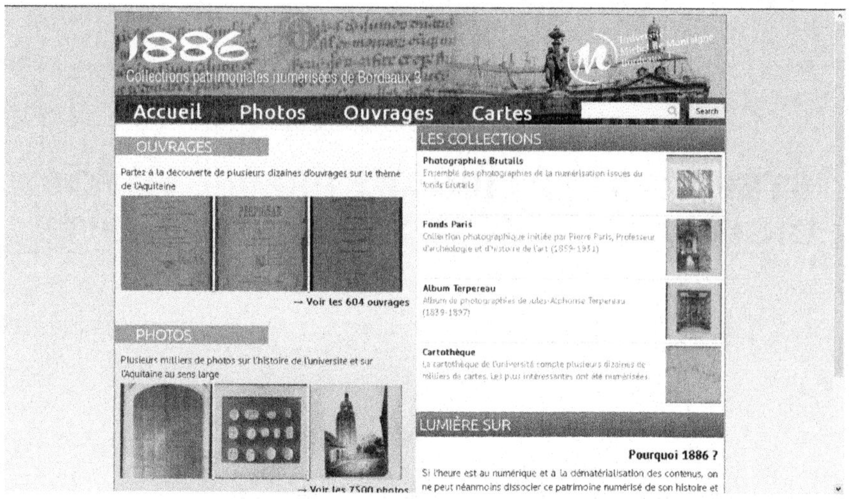

Figure 5.1. Omeka Example Site. ***Website capture. Digital Image. 1886—Collections Patrimoniales Numérisées De Bordeaux 3. Omeka RSS. http://1886.u-bordeaux3.fr***

updates and maintenance performed by the hosted service. Since Omeka does all the work maintaining your site, this is an excellent choice for our project and for beginners.

Begin your Omeka project by going to Omeka.net and clicking on the Sign Up button. Choose the free basic plan. You will be asked to create a username. This is the name you will you use to access your account, it is not the name of your site. Additional information for signing up are first and last name, password creation, and e-mail address. Once all the information is entered correctly, you must agree to the terms of service (http://info.omeka.net/terms-of-service/) and enter the CAPTCHA.

After creating an account, you will receive an e-mail with an activation link. You must click on that link in order to activate your account. Failure to do so will result in the account being removed. The activation link is one-time use. Once you click on it, you will be taken to Omeka.net where your account will be activated. You are now ready to log in to your account.

Log in to your account using the username and password you created. Upon logging in, you will be on My Dashboard, where you will see that you currently have the basic plan, using zero of one sites and using 0 MB of 500 MB of storage space. Now it is time to add a site.

Site Set Up

Click on the Add a Site button to the right of the dashboard. Here you will add the subdomain, title, and description. The subdomain will include the domain *.omeka.net* after it. For example, suppose the name I want to choose is *abclibraryexhibit.* The subdomain and URL that visitors will use to access my site will be *abclibraryexhibit.omeka.net.* When choosing a name, try to keep it simple yet descriptive. Either include the abbreviation of your institution or a condensed version. Also try to include the exhibits title. Here is an actual example:

> http://jdenzeronlineexhibit.omeka.net/

After you add the site, you can visit, manage, or delete the site from My Dashboard. Click on Visit Site to see the site up and running. You will notice that there is a title and no content. The layout is a default theme. Now you can configure, change the look and feel, and add site users. I will go through the steps to add a collection and some items.

Begin by clicking on Manage Site from My Dashboard. This will take you to the main dashboard. This is the main control panel where you will update and manage your site. The My Dashboard is a brief overview of your site and only has the functionality to view, edit, and delete a site. For the remainder of the project, you will work with the main dashboard. Access it by clicking on Manage Site from My Dashboard.

The first thing you are going to want to do is configure your Omeka site. Click on Settings, which is located on the top menu bar next to Users. The General tab will have the administrator e-mail, title, and description that has already been set. If these need to be updated, here is where you could change them. Make sure to enter the copyright information and author information of the site as well as any tags separated by a comma delimiter. Be sure to save your changes so they take effect.

Themes

Next we are going to change the theme of your site. At the top menu, click on Appearance. Change your theme to Rhythm by clicking Use this Theme. The theme will be changed as soon as you click that link. Let's configure the theme by clicking on Configure Theme. Try changing the style sheet to Spring Rhythm. Now you will add your own logo for the site. Browse to the image file you want to use by clicking on the Browse button under the logo file. Choose a file that is either a JPG, GIF, or PNG. The file cannot be larger than 300 KB in size, and it should not exceed 500 pixels in width. Add a site tagline, which will be the text that appears under the heading. Add some footer text, which can be formatted with HTML or not. Enter some Home Page text, this also can be HTML or not. The Home Page text will be displayed under the Browse Items menu. Once all the setting are made, click on Save Changes and the changes will be applied.

Add Users

Now let's add some users to the site. Adding users is a great way to manage and update your site. This will allow the site to have several levels of contributors and administrators. This is not the same as site visitors. Those type of users should not have access to your site. Omeka allows the following types of users.

- Super: Access to the entire site and all settings.
- Admin: All access without control of settings.
- Researcher: View items and collections that are not public.
- Contributor: Can tag, add, edit, and delete items. Can create exhibits from public items. Can see items that are not public. Cannot make their own items public.

Create at least one account for admin, researcher, and contributor. These accounts can be deleted or changed in the future.

Your Omeka site is now configured with the basic settings. Now you can begin to create a collection and add items to the collection.

Create a Collection

To begin creating a collection, click on Collections to the left of the dashboard. Click on the Add a Collection button to create a new collection. Fill out all the needed metadata. Each text area can be HTML code by checking the Use HTML checkbox. Once all of the metadata fields are populated, check the Public checkbox to make it available for all to see. Optionally, the Featured checkbox can be checked, which will add the collection to the featured section on the main page of your site.

Now that the collection has been created, it is time to add some images and link them to your collection. Start by clicking on Add a New Item link to create the metadata and add any files. Begin with a simple image file. Fill in all of the necessary metadata just as you would a collection from the steps above. Next add the image file for this item by clicking on the Files link from the menu on the page. Select Choose a File and browse to the image file you want to add. You can add more than one file per new item. Select the file type. You can choose from several file types and you can also create new file types. Once the metadata are entered and the file is selected, select your collection to add the item using the dropdown menu. Check Public, and finish adding it by clicking Add Item. Add about ten more items to your collection by repeating the steps above.

Your Omeka site is now ready to be viewed by all. There are several other settings and themes to use; don't be afraid to experiment. The site is designed so that you virtually cannot break it. Additionally, there is documentation and a forum to find help if you need it (http://omeka.org/codex/Documentation and http://omeka.org/forums/). The next section will discuss some of the exciting plug-ins that will help to enhance your site and digital exhibit. Plug-ins are not required to run your site, but they are highly recommended and easy to install.

Omeka Plug-Ins: Which to Choose

Like many open-source content management systems such as MediaWiki, Wordpress, or Joomla that offer plug-ins, Omeka has a great number of plug-ins that extend the basic functionality of the CMS. These extensions are very flexible and customizable. This allows for much more control of your Omeka site. Plug-ins can also be created by anyone, which offers even more flexibility for your site. Omeka plug-ins are easy to install, configure, and manage. This section will discuss the best plug-ins to start with for those new to Omeka.

Installing a plug-in is extremely easy in Omeka. First click on Manage Site and then go to the dashboard. Click on Plugins from the top menu. Select Install on the plug-in you wish to activate. Depending on the plug-in, you may have to enter some additional information to configure it. Uninstalling the plug-in is as easy as clicking Deactivate. You can always choose to reactivate any plug-in.

The free account on Omeka only offers thirteen plug-ins; upgraded accounts offer more, and self-hosted sites are unlimited. The following plug-ins have been chosen for both ease and best choice when starting with Omeka:

- CSV Import
- Docs Viewer
- Exhibit Builder
- Google Analytics
- PDF Embed
- LC Suggest

CSV Import is a great plug-in that allows you to import items from a simple CSV file (comma-separated values). Each row in your CSV file will contain metadata for one item. This makes it easier to create new items without having to manually enter all the metadata. Microsoft Excel is a great tool for creating CSV files. Spreadsheets are easily readable when using Excel, and exporting them to a CSV is simple. Additional information on using CSV Import is available at http://omeka.org/codex/Plugins/CSV_Import_2.0.

Docs Viewer is a plug-in that should be a default in Omeka. Google Docs are widely used by Internet users. Adding this viewer to view Google Docs just makes sense. This takes the guesswork out of the visitor's browser to either download or try to open the item. Nothing is more frustrating to a user than having to install a plug-in to view a file. The plug-in allows you to enable or disable the viewer for both admin and public items. The width and height of the viewer is also configurable.

Exhibit Builder is probably the most useful plug-in when starting this project. It will help you get started on your first exhibit by making the data entry as well as adding pages easier. Creating an exhibit through the dashboard is not complex, but for a first-time user, it may be a bit too much at first. That is why Exhibit Builder makes it simple. The exhibits may be either one page or multiple pages. For more information on how to configure and use the plug-in, visit http://omeka.org/codex/Plugins/ExhibitBuilder_3.0.

Google Analytics is another simple plug-in that should be a default on Omeka. Librarians know how important statistics are in libraries. Google Analytics is a great way to track and get statistics on your site. If you are not familiar with Google Analytics, check out http://www.google.com/analytics/. Then you can also create or access your account. Configuring the plug-in is simple, just add your Google Analytics account ID. If you do not know your ID, you can access it by following these steps:

1. Create or log in to you Google Analytics account.
2. Add a Website Profile for your Omeka.net website.
3. Copy the value for the account ID found next to the site URL (starts with UA-).

PDF Embed is just like the Docs Viewer plug-in, except it uses the PDF format. PDFs are an industry standard. Adding support that handles how a PDF item should open makes it easier for the visitor. The plug-in allows you to set the in-browser viewer plug-in for PDFs, or you can choose a cross-platform JavaScript viewer. Choosing the JavaScript viewer is the safest way to ensure that the PDF will be viewed without issues. But since PDFs are standard, almost every Internet user has some sort of plug-in installed. So selecting the in-browser option is the best choice. The plug-in also allows you to configure the height of the PDF viewer. The width is automatically adjusted in proportion to the height.

LC Suggest is a plug-in that adds an autocomplete feature to almost any metadata field in your Omeka site. It pulls results from the Library of Congress's list of authorities and controlled vocabularies. This will help to ensure that your Omeka site is consistent with metadata input and that the data are compatible with other databases of records. More information is available at http://omeka.org/codex/Plugins/Library_of_Congress_Suggest_2.0.

Here are a few more plug-ins that are available with a paid or upgraded account that librarians might be interested in:

Dublin Core Extended is important to add to your Omeka site because it adds extended Dublin Core properties to the Dublin Core element set.

Bulk Metadata Editor offers a quick and easy way to search and update metadata in fields. This is quite useful in managing your Omeka collection of items. Installation is simple and does not require an extensive configuration.

HOW TO CREATE A HANDS-FREE DIGITAL EXHIBIT SHOWCASE WITH MICROSOFT KINECT

We have all seen those exciting exhibits where patrons are able to walk up to a digital display and interact seamlessly with it. You see them in museums and libraries. Some are as small as an average tablet; others can be as large as an entire wall. Users interact with content full of images, text, videos, and sound, all of which is nonlinear. They can go back and forth and jump to any section of a display. They find themselves immersed in a digital world of sight and sound, enabling them to navigate and explore these worlds at their own pace and comfort.

Imagine being able to provide that user experience in your own library or museum without having an elaborate setup. Imagine a hands-free digital exhibit that is just as good as or even better than most high-end touchscreens at a fraction of the cost with virtually no maintenance.

By now the thought of adding a hands-free digital exhibit has you excited. With the barriers of cost and maintenance removed, you are free to explore exciting possibilities, such as the kind of content you would like to use and where you might want to place the exhibit. You can even start to imagine how users are going to enjoy the digital exhibit experience.

Along with this excitement, though, there is probably one question in the back of your mind. You are asking yourself, "Can I do it?" You might have some doubts, questioning whether you have the skills needed to accomplish this project. Let me put that doubt to rest. If you can install a digital display such as a large flat-screen monitor or projector, install software on a Windows computer, and create content using basic HTML or a CMS such as Wordpress, then this project is for you.

Setting up a hands-free digital exhibit with Microsoft Kinect is ideal for beginners, but advanced users will quickly see how they can create stunning digital exhibits without investing too much time and effort on the hands-free portion of the project. Although most hands-free applications require a significant investment in time and effort, using Kinect will allow you to maximize your development skills. You will learn how and where to place the Kinect for the best results, how to choose the right digital display, install and configure the software needed to have a hands-free digital exhibit, and create a simple user interface for your digital exhibit.

Location

Before you can begin to create a hands-free digital display, you have to evaluate the space to determine the best location for your setup. Although you may think location is not nearly as important as the choice in hardware and software, choosing the ideal spot is crucial when creating a digital exhibit. There are many variables that will affect the hands-free experience. It is these variables that can turn what you intended to be a great user experience into an experience that may frustrate your patrons. In addition, this kind of negative reaction could discourage you from attempting to create future hands-free exhibits.

So let's avoid that pitfall from the beginning and choose the proper location. When choosing a location, you should consider the following:

- Location size
- Lighting
- Visibility
- Traffic
- Data and electrical ports
- Mounting surfaces

Location Size

Choosing the location for the digital exhibit is not limited to deciding where the display will be mounted. You must consider the location of the Kinect and the computer and their relative distance from the display. For instance, the Kinect requires a minimum distance from the display in order to work properly. In addition, the computer may need to draw both data and power from a source that is not conveniently close to the display.

Think about what your budget will allow in terms of the size of your display. If you are only able to budget low-range displays (thirty-two to thirty-seven inches), then avoid using an area such as a lobby. The large open area will diminish your display, and users will be less drawn to it. Of course, if your display will be part of a much larger physical exhibit that incorporates props, then using such a large area may not be a big issue. Be careful of using too small a display in a large area.

Just as choosing a large area for a small display is not recommended, choosing a small area to house a large display is not advised either. The idea that bigger is always better doesn't apply here. If the area you are going to use is similar to a small, 12- by 18-foot conference room, then using a large sixty-inch or bigger display is not ideal. Users may feel overwhelmed or intimidated by a large display in a small area. Proper balance is key.

Lighting

Lighting for the hands-free digital exhibit is not restricted to simply making content visible to users. It is important for the Kinect, which will be powering the user interface (UI). Although the Kinect works in low light, you should make sure the area is properly lit to ensure that the Kinect is able to communicate the UI with better accuracy. Failing to provide enough light will cause the Kinect's tracking system to experience lag or loss of tracking. On the other hand, too much lighting will have similar results. Ensure that direct lighting is not aimed toward the Kinect.

It is important to take these considerations into account before starting your project. Once you have chosen an area, you may not have the option to move or change the lighting. A good example of this is fixed lighting such as ceiling "can" lights, since replacing or moving them may not be in your budget. Plan ahead to avoid setbacks.

Visibility and Patron Traffic

Just as lighting is important, so too is visibility. Make sure your display is placed where the greatest number of users will be exposed to it. Because it will also be used as an attention-grabbing, noninteractive display when it is not being used, do not limit its use by putting it in a corner. At the same time, avoid placing it in a high-traffic area where users don't have time to stop and interact with it. Make sure you are grabbing the attention of patrons entering the building instead of exiting; those on their way out may not have time to stop, and your impact will be lost. Keep the visibility of your hands-free digital exhibit in mind when choosing the perfect location.

Data and Electrical Ports

Your digital display will need at least one power source for the equipment running your setup. Power will be needed for the display, the Kinect, and the computer running the software. Depending on your setup, you may need more than one power source. For example, suppose you have decided to use a flat-panel display. The Kinect and the display will each require separate power outlets. Both of them will be placed opposite each other. Powering them from one side is not possible without having to run cables, which is unsightly.

It is also important to keep the display uncluttered by minimizing the amount of cable running. You can't avoid a cable running from your computer to the display without investing in an expensive wireless display. Locating the Kinect and computer near the same power source of the display, in order to avoid using additional power sources, will create excessive cable clutter. This will make it less appealing and difficult to disguise.

If your hands-free digital exhibit will connect to an external web server, make sure there is a data-line network connection near the power source. Although you can run your presentation off a wireless connection using your institution's wireless connection, it is not recommended. Hard-wired connections offer better connection stability than WiFi.

Mounting

Finally, when choosing a location, make sure that you survey the area in terms of ease of installation. Check with the institution's maintenance department to ensure that you are able to mount your display and install any shelving or cases needed to house your equipment. It would be a shame to choose the perfect location only to have your plans stopped because the maintenance department says it is not possible.

Digital Display

Just as choosing the right location is key, choosing the right, balanced display is also important. You should look into the following when choosing a digital display:

- Screen size
- Physical weight and size
- Resolution
- Type of display

Screen Size

First, let's consider the best screen size to use. Screen size does not refer to the actual size of the display you are using. Instead, screen size refers to the viewable display of the content, minus any casing or non-displayable areas. Screen size is measured diagonally from corner to corner of the inside of the bezel. If you are using a projector, screen size is measured by the actual viewing area being projected and is still measured diagonally.

Look at the location you have chosen for your digital exhibit. If the area is going to have a wall-mounted or wall-projected area, measure the wall. Make sure you have enough room to mount or project your area. Ensure plenty of wall space surrounding the display, so you can add physical signs and props next to the display. Such extras will help draw attention to the display, making it more inviting and welcoming. Consider these items when choosing the size and remember: Bigger is not always better.

If you choose a non-wall-mounted display, be sure to choose a screen size that does not interfere with the flow of traffic in the area.

You don't want to have a large display that will create a bottleneck effect. Also make sure you choose a display that allows plenty of viewing distance.

Your digital exhibit is not only going to be an interactive display, it is also going to be a noninteractive display when it is not in use. Other patrons passing by will find themselves looking at the content and enjoying your display. This viewable distance is very important. Make sure there is plenty of distance for users to step back and take in the full exhibit. If you decide to make a seventy-inch display, take into account that users will have to step back to view it. The viewing distance for a seventy-inch display is about 8.75 to 14.75 feet. Don't overwhelm or confine users when they are interacting with your display. Remember, the goal of your digital display is to give users the control to navigate and explore the digital exhibits at their own pace and comfort.

Physical Size and Weight

Now that you have chosen a screen size, let's look at the physical size and weight of your display. Today's displays have become so thin and light that we no longer are limited to using bulky displays and disguising them with creative props. If you are going to mount your display on a wall, be sure to take into account the size and weight of the display when determining whether the wall can support it. Some walls may be made of materials that are prohibitive to mounting. Ensure that the physical dimensions do not make the mounted display unsafe. Remember, although this is a hands-free device, users will inevitably tap on the display.

Some displays may require proper ventilation, which will require installing them some distance from the wall. This might add to the bulk of your setup, which may not be part of your initial vision. Go to your local technology store and look at their display, if possible. This will help you get an idea of the actual size of a display, as it is common to be disappointed with the reality of a display you have only seen on the Internet. Of course, the actual physical size and weight of the display will not be an issue if you are using a projector.

Resolution

Now that you have chosen the screen size and physical size, it is important to choose the right resolution. You are creating a digital exhibit, so your content will be full of rich text, images, and videos. Common high-definition resolutions are 1280-by-720, 1366-by-768, and 1920-by-1080 pixels. The most commonly used are 1366-by-768 and 1920-by-1080 pixels. For best performance, it is recommend that you use 1920-by-1080 pixels. Also make sure that the computer you will be using to run the exhibit is capable of that resolution.

Type of Display

Finally, consider the type of display that is best for your application. There are basically two types of displays you will choose from. One is the flat-panel display, which is the high-definition plasma, LCD, and LED television screens. Flat-panel displays are suited for areas where lighting is both bright and dim, since the brightness can be adjusted. If mounted correctly, they give the install a cleaner, more professional look. However, flat-panel displays have limitations. Once you choose a size, you are confined to that size until you buy a new display. If your exhibit expands or changes location and requires a larger screen, you will not be able to simply increase the size as you could with a projector. Flat-panel displays are also limited to where they can be mounted. Special care must be given to the displays. For example, suppose you want to display your exhibit as a flat table. Using a flat panel is not recommended because users tend to not be very careful. Flat panels are not designed for users to lean on as they would a table. Flat panels may also be too heavy for certain surfaces, such as portable partitions.

The second type of display is the projector. Projectors are great for digital exhibits because they come in various sizes that make them easy to set up and project. You can find high-quality projectors that are as small as a deck of cards. They are also versatile in scalability. You will find that you can increase or decrease the projected size just by moving the projector. Compared to flat-panel displays, they are less expensive relative to screen size. Projectors can also be projected onto virtually any flat surface. This allows you to project them onto a table.

However, projectors also have limitations. Too much lighting may make it difficult to see projected images. Some projectors may only work well in low light, which will be a problem when using the Kinect. Projectors require a certain distance to project the digital exhibit, which may not be feasible in your spaces. Even with the more expensive, high-end, short-throw projectors, a minimum distance is still required to project images effectively. Projectors must be properly angled so that users are not blocking the projected display, which can be difficult with many setups.

The choice of a flat-panel display or projector will depend on the budget of the project as well as the chosen area. Each type has its own pros and cons. More details on choosing a flat panel or projector can be read in chapter 6.

Potential of Microsoft Kinect

Since Microsoft introduced the Xbox Kinect in November of 2010, hackers and do-it-yourselfers have been fascinated by its potential. Hackers were quickly able to "hack" into the Kinect, allowing it to transcend its beginnings as a gaming-system peripheral.

Developers found that the Kinect had potential in many applications beyond gaming, from simple image capturing to real-time object tracking. Microsoft recognized this development wave and decided to release a software development kit (SDK) for the Xbox 360 and Windows versions of the Kinect.

With this release of the SDK, developers began to create several open-source applications that used the Kinect. Developers also recognized a market for hands-free interactive displays. It is precisely this "hack" that will allow you to harness the power of the Kinect to use in your hands-free digital exhibit.

Why use the Kinect? Isn't it just a device for gaming? Initially it was developed for gaming, but developers have found many more uses for it. The Kinect is a great low-cost alternative to expensive touchscreen displays and is just as easy to use and install. Although it may not have the precision of a high-end touchscreen, the intent of this project is not to create a highly precise display, but rather an innovative, attention-drawing one.

The Kinect has two options: the original Xbox 360 Kinect and the Kinect for Windows. The Kinect for Windows also comes in the original Xbox 360 style Version 1 and now the upgraded Version 2. Version 2 has various improvements, and its look is similar to the new Xbox One Kinect. The Xbox 360 version is for development only, but it will work with that software for this project. The Kinect for Windows is licensed for commercial use.

Choosing the best version will depend on your budget. Table 5.1 will help you make the right decision for your application.

If your budget is limited, you may be using an existing display and unable to afford the $149 to $199 cost for one of the Windows versions (prices are at the time of writing). In that case, you may decide to use the lower-priced Xbox 360 version. Used models can be found in gaming stores, such as GameStop, for around $40. Note that the Xbox 360 Kinect being sold at these stores comes in two versions. One includes the AC adapter and one does not. The one that does not have the AC adapter will not work on your Windows computer. It uses a proprietary port to connect to the Xbox 360. Make sure you get the version that has the AC adapter and connects via a USB port.

If your budget will allow it, I strongly recommend purchasing the Kinect for Windows, Version 2, since the pricing is the same for both Windows versions. Note that Version 2 will only work with Windows 8 and 8.1. The high-end software, UBI Interactive, that we are going to use in this application is compatible with Kinect Version 2 as well as Windows 8 and 8.1. The Kinect for Windows may be purchased directly from Microsoft at www.microsoftstore.com. They offer free shipping and free returns. You can also get academic pricing for the Kinect.

Once you have purchased the Kinect, you will have to install the drivers for the device and connect it to your computer. You will need to install the SDK for the Kinect from Microsoft www.microsoft.com/en-us/kinectforwindows. If you are using V2, make sure to download SDK 2.0. If you will be using Xbox 360 or V1, make sure to download SDK 1.8. Each version supports only its specific SDK. Once you have downloaded the SDK, follow these install instructions. To install the SDK:

Table 5.1.

	Xbox 360	**Kinect for Windows V1**	**Kinect for Windows V2**
Version	Original Xbox 360	Version 1	Version 2 (latest)
Hardware	Original Processor	Original Processor	Version 2 processor
License	Developer	Commercial	Commercial
Price	$40 Used	$199 Commercial $149 Academic	$199 Commercial $149 Academic
Compatibility	Windows 7 Windows 8, 8.1	Windows 7 Windows 8, 8.1	Windows 8, 8.1

1. Make sure the Kinect sensor is not plugged into any of the USB ports on the computer.
2. Remove any other drivers for the Kinect sensor.
3. From the download location, double-click on the Kinect setup file. This single installer works for both 32-bit and 64-bit Windows.
4. Once the SDK has completed installing successfully, ensure the Kinect sensor is plugged into an external power source and then plug the Kinect sensor into the PC's USB port. The drivers will load automatically.
5. The Kinect sensor should now be working correctly.

Once the Kinect is installed, it is time to mount it, either above or below your display. For this project, the ideal location is above, in order to ensure that the Kinect is not touched by users. Exact placement will be discussed in the UI section of this project.

Software

The Kinect software you will be using is a commercial product. Open-source software is available, but it's too limited for this project. In order to get the best user experience, it is best to use a commercial product. This project will offer you two software options to choose from: one low-priced software and the other a high-priced product.

Touchless Touch (low end)

The Touchless Touch system costs only $59.99. It offers a 128-point touch system that can handle displays over 200 inches. It is appropriate for both flat-panel and projected displays. Anywhere you can project a display, the Touchless Touch can make it interactive. The software is straightforward. The actual placement of the Kinect may not be ideal or aesthetically pleasing for a digital exhibit, because unlike with the usual display for gaming, in order to create a digital exhibit with this application, the Kinect must be placed diagonally and a few feet from the display. The system is capable of connecting four Kinects simultaneously, adding better accuracy. However, because the digital displays in this project will be used for navigation of the exhibit, there is no need for precise interaction, making the use of four Kinects excessive. Note that only one Kinect for Windows Version 2 can be connected at one time.

Let's begin with the installation of the software. First, download the software from Touchless at www.touchlesstouch.com/touchlesstouch.zip. Make sure the Kinect is NOT connected to the computer:

1. Note that Touchless Touch supports only the Kinect Xbox 360 and V1.
2. Extract the contents of the zip file to a separate folder on the computer.
3. Run the *setup.exe* file.
4. Follow the prompts in the install process.
5. If you have not already installed the Kinect SDK, the install will install it for you.
6. Once the install process is complete, connect the Kinect.
7. Double-click on the Touchless Touch icon in the lower-right corner to begin calibration.

Next, you will need to mount the Kinect. Mounting the Kinect may be different from your expectations, if you have seen the Kinect in action. Because the Kinect is not tracking the actual user's movement or gestures, like that of the Xbox 360 gaming system, the Kinect will not face the user. Instead, it will run as parallel to the touch surface as possible. This is done to achieve better tracking. This also limits your tracking view to about fifty-eight degrees. The sensor must be as flat and close to the flat surface as possible. Place the Kinect at a minimum distance of forty centimeters from the flat surface and four meters from the corner of the projected display. Place it diagonal to the display (figure 5.2).

Once the placement of the Kinect is done, you would begin the calibration. Double-click on the Touchless Touch icon in the lower-right corner to bring up the console. You will see the Kinect listed as device one. A green light in the control panel will indicate it is connected. Click on Calibrate Devices, which will start the calibration process. Click on Begin Calibration. The software will run a series of tests to check for background noise for the Kinect and display. After about a minute, you will be prompted to touch the screen for calibration. Touch and hold each touchscreen crosshair point. When the point is regis-

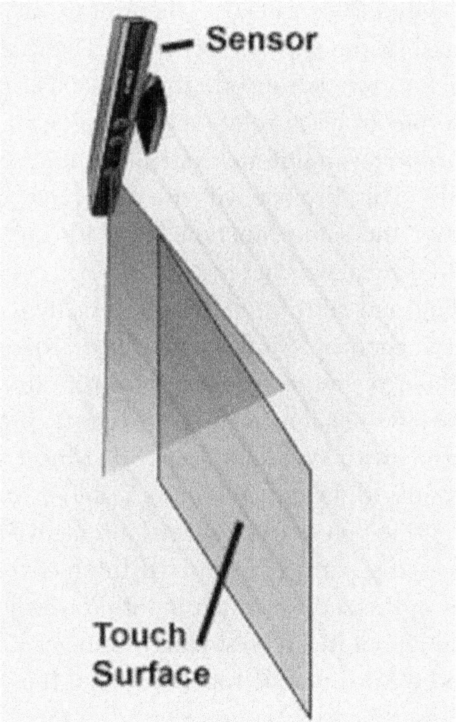

Figure 5.2. Touchless Touch Kinect Alignment. ***Image courtesy of Rob Smith. www.touchlesstouch.com***

tered, it will move to the next point. Continue until you have touched all points. Once you are done, calibration is complete and the Kinect is ready for interaction. Interaction will be similar to using a mouse.

UBI Interactive (high end)

The alternative to Touchless Touch is UBI Interactive (www.ubi-interactive.com). This software is much easier to set up and calibrate than Touchless Touch and offers greater functionality, taking advantage of Windows 8 and Windows 8.1 touch input capabilities. The price is much more than Touchless Touch, but it will fit most budgets, and academic pricing is available. Pricing as of this writing is listed in table 5.2.

For entry-level hands-free digital exhibits, the Basic and Professional versions are well suited. This will allow the user to navigate through the display, clicking and swiping between content. The Business and Enterprise versions are for more advanced exhibits, such as using both hands to connect puzzle pieces or to rotate and zoom an image. The Enterprise edition incorporates multitouch and allows multiple users to interact simultaneously. This project will use the Basic and Professional versions. Both offer the same functionality, with the only differences being in maximum display size and price.

Before installing and setting up UBI Interactive, be sure you are using the correct version of Windows with your Kinect. As noted before, this project allows you to use any version of the Kinect, but the software and Windows version must be matched up correctly. Kinect V2 is only compatible with Windows 8 and 8.1. Kinect V1 and Xbox 360 version are both compatible with Windows 7, and 8, and 8.1. Note that Windows 7 will require you to use a special interactive pen. The special pen can be purchased separately from UBI Interactive. This is because Windows 7 is not optimized for touch input. You will have hands-free interactive capability, but it will be similar to using a mouse. Windows 8 and 8.1 are geared toward mobile touch displays. It is recommend that you use Kinect V1 or V2 and Windows 8 or 8.1.

Now that you have matched the Kinect to your Windows operating system, you can install the software. This project uses Kinect V2 and Windows 8.1. The installation is similar for all other versions of Kinect and Windows 7, so don't worry if you have chosen to use a different version.

First, download and obtain an activation code from UBI. UBI offers a free, thirty-day limited trial. Once you have downloaded and obtained the license code, install the software. Follow the prompts to install UBI Interactive and enter your activation code. If you are using a trial, the

Table 5.2.

	Basic	**Professional**	**Business**	**Enterprise**
Touch Type	Single Point	Single Point	Multi-Touch Point	Multi-Touch Point
Gestures	Tap, Swipe	Tap, Swipe	Tap, Swipe, Zoom	Tap, Swipe, Zoom
Max. Display Size	45"	120"	120"	120"
Price	$149	$379	$799	$1499

activation code will be e-mailed to you upon your trial request. The install process will prompt you to disable the right-click mode to enhance performance.

Once the software is installed, connect the Kinect and calibrate the system. Plug in the Kinect AC adapter and connect the USB end of the Kinect to your computer. Make sure that the Kinect is plugged into a dedicated USB. This is a USB port that is directly connected to the computer and not a USB hub that connects several devices.

After you have successfully connected the Kinect, you are ready to launch the UBI software. Launch UBI by pressing the Windows key, then typing UBI. Windows 7 users will launch the program by going to the Start menu. Once the program is launched, you will be prompted to calibrate the system.

UBI's default profile settings are designed for projected surfaces. There is a workaround for flat-panel displays. We will begin calibration with the easier projected display. First, position the Kinect far enough from the projected surface. The minimum distance is approximately three feet. If you are not using a short-throw projector, the ideal position is near the projector or mounted directly on top of or beneath the projector. The UBI software will let you know if the Kinect is too close. You will have to adjust the position so that the entire display is visible to the Kinect. You can adjust the angle of the Kinect using the track-bar slider. DO NOT try to manually adjust the Kinect by moving the arm up and down. Doing so will damage the internal gears (figure 5.3).

Once the Kinect is in position and the entire display is visible, you are ready to calibrate. Click Start and the calibration will begin. You will see a pattern of black dots on a white background. The calibration will take a few seconds. Once the calibration is complete, you are ready to interact with the display. Unlike Touchless Touch, UBI Interactive does not use any touch-points grids. It is a one-button calibration process.

As noted before, UBI's default profile is set for projected displays. Getting UBI Interactive to work on a flat panel requires a workaround. Below are the instructions on how to calibrate a flat-panel display:

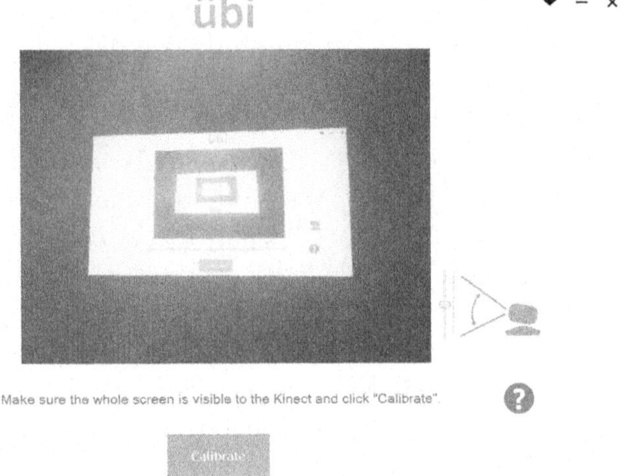

Figure 5.3. UBI Calibration. ***Calibration set up. Digital Image. Make the World Your Touchscreen. UBI Interactive. http://www.ubi-interactive.com***

1. First download the custom LCD profile: forum.ubi-interactive.com/hc/en-us/article_attachments/200835616/LCD_TV.zip.
2. Extract the zip file to a location on your computer.
3. Run the *install_profile* file.
4. Make sure the Kinect is set up and connected.
5. Run the UBI Interactive program.
6. Make sure the entire screen is visible by the Kinect.
7. Click Calibrate.
8. Cover the entire screen with white paper, making sure the paper is flush against the screen.
9. Click Depth Calib.
10. Remove the white paper.

User Interface

Now that you have the Kinect and the hands-free software installed, you can prepare your digital exhibit content for viewing and interaction. The content that users will be interacting with should be the only thing they see. You don't want users accessing other programs and features on the computer. In order to restrict this, you will need to put the computer into kiosk mode.

If you are running Windows 8 or 8.1, you are going to have to disable the Windows Charm Bar. The Windows Charm Bar is a Windows menu that is activated when a user hovers over a hotspot with the pointer. The Charm menu allows users to turn off, restart, and search for programs on their computer. You don't want them to have that level of access to the computer. To disable the Charm Bar:

1. Right-click the task bar and click Properties.
2. Click on the Navigation tab.
3. Uncheck the following: "When I point to the upper-right corner, show the charms" and "When I click on the upper-left corner, switch between my recent apps."
4. Click OK and the Charm Bar will be disabled.

After the Charm Bar is disabled, you will want to run a program to put the exhibit into kiosk mode. A simple and easy solution is to run Internet Explorer in kiosk mode. Kiosk mode runs the browser in full screen without any access to menus and toolbars. Because the computer is not attached to a keyboard, you will not have to worry about anyone accessing the hotkeys or the Windows key. Such key functions can give users access to the computer.

To enter Internet Explorer into kiosk mode:

1. Click on the Windows Start button.
2. Click Run.
3. Type in the following: **iexplore–k *page*** (where *page* is the web address you want Internet Explorer to navigate to). For example: **iexplore–k www.binghamton.edu/libraries**
4. If you want Internet Explorer to navigate to an HTML page on the computer, use the following example: **iexplore–k "c:\my documents\My Exhibit.html"**

If you want to automate this and add it to your startup folder, create a batch file:

1. Open Notepad.
2. Type in the following: **"C:\Program Files\Internet Explorer\iexplore.exe" -k *page*** where *page* is the web address you want Internet Explorer to navigate to.

3. Save the batch file as "*kioskmode.bat*". Make sure to include the double quotation marks.
4. Double-click on that file to launch kiosk mode.
5. To exit Internet Explorer kiosk mode, press the **Alt** and **F4** keys.

The digital exhibit may be an existing online exhibit that you have already created. Keep in mind that the hands-free digital exhibit will use touch to interact, so you will have to reevaluate the way users navigate on the existing exhibit. Links and buttons should be enlarged to accommodate touch. Users may become frustrated if you have them click on small links and buttons. Users should be able to navigate with a smooth and natural motion.

If you do not have an online web exhibit, you can easily create one for free. The first project in this chapter is an example. Once you have created your Omeka site, you are going to want to make sure the web browser is in full-screen kiosk mode. All three popular web browsers—Internet Explorer, Firefox, and Chrome—have full-screen mode. Each can be placed in full-screen mode by pressing **F11** on the keyboard. This will launch the browser with no toolbars or status bars. The entire web page will be in view. The best browser to use is Chrome because it will only allow you to exit full-screen mode by pressing F11. The other two browsers will actually give you the menu bar if you touch the top of the page. This will allow users to exit your digital exhibit, which is something you don't want. If you are using Windows 8 or 8.1, you can go to the Windows store and download Kiosk SP Browser. This app will run a browser in actual kiosk mode, which is preferred over using Chrome. Windows 7 users cannot download and use Kiosk SP Browser.

CREATE A DIGITAL EXHIBIT USING OPEN EXHIBITS

Do you remember the last time you entered a museum and came across an exhibit that used digital content such as text and images in an exciting way? The exhibit seemed to use software that was either specifically designed for the exhibit or would be too expensive. Maybe it was beyond the scope of your expertise? If there were only something that is easy to use, free, and exciting. Well, there is, and it is called Open Exhibits (OE).

Open Exhibits is a framework, that is, a collection of software tools that allows you to create a touch-interactive exhibit. This can be used in museums and other cultural institutions, enabling its users to actively engage with a digital exhibit. Unlike the previous project, which can be used with any type of application that incorporates touch, Open Exhibits projects are specific to the online exhibit type they are designed to be. For example, one of the projects is Museum Timeline. This allows you to create your own timeline with specific attributes. It is funded and sponsored by the National Science Foundation (NSF). Open Exhibits is unique in that it provides more than just a single specific software program; instead it has a combination of parts that you bring together to create a digital exhibit. It offers a suite of shared, dynamic open-source tools that you can use, developed by a growing community of collaborators who bring cutting-edge technologies to digital exhibits. This project will guide you through how to set up a digital open exhibit. In this project you will learn how to:

- Create an Open Exhibits account.
- Choose the right hardware to get started.
- Download and install the Open Exhibits Player 1.1, OE SDK, and Adobe Flash Player Projector.
- Set up your software environment and download exhibit files.
- Customize the following exhibit with your own content:

  a. Museum Timeline
  b. Album Exhibit
  c. Moon Gigapixel
  d. Hurricane Sandy Before & After

Creating an Open Exhibits Account

Open Exhibits requires creating an account. Creating an account is quick and easy. There is no lengthy sign-up process.

It is important that you use your real name when creating an account. Open Exhibits periodically checks for spammers, and any name that may appears fake to them will be removed. Also, all fields are required, including the URL of your institution. You will also be asked for a brief statement of intent.

When you fill out the statement of intent, make sure to provide as much detail about your intended use for Open Exhibits. This helps the community members know what your contributions will be for Open Exhibits. Although you are not required to contribute to the community, providing a clear statement will help your institution when asking for support from the community. This is also a great way for community members to reach out to other institutions that may have similar interests. Consideration for an SDK license requires that you include your institution's name.

Choose the Best Hardware to Set Up an Exhibit

Choosing the best hardware for your Open Exhibits depends on your budget. Open Exhibits takes advantage of touchscreen technology. So the hardware that will be needed is a touchscreen display, such as a tablet device. If you cannot afford a touchscreen display due to the limited budget, you can use the project above titled "How to Create Your Own Hands-Free Digital Exhibit Showcase with the Microsoft Kinect." There you will learn how to install your own touchscreen display using the Microsoft Kinect. The project is low cost and will fit most limited budgets.

If your budget allows for a touchscreen display, it is recommended to use a multipoint touch display. This will allow you to take advantage of the power of the Open Exhibits and add-ons. Open Exhibits is compatible with Windows 8 and 8.1. Both versions of Windows were designed around touch input, so for this project I will be using 8.1, along with a Windows 8.1 touch-enabled, all-in-one, or any computer that has a touch-enabled screen, flat-display computer.

Open Exhibits Player 1.1, OE SDK, and Adobe Flash Player Projector

After you have created your new Open Exhibits account, log in and download the Open Exhibits Player 1.1 at http://openexhibits.org/downloads. The player requires Adobe Air, which can be downloaded at http://get.adobe.com/air. Install the Adobe Air first. The player will not allow you to install it before Air is installed. Once you have downloaded the player:

1. Extract the contents into a separate folder.
2. Double-click on the file *OE-Player-1.1.air.*
3. Adobe Air will step you though the install process.
4. Click on the Install button.
5. Click Continue to install the player.
6. When the install process is complete, the player will launch.
7. Exit the player by clicking on File, then Exit.

Next, download the OE SDK 4.1 at http://openexhibits.org/downloads:

1. Extract the SDK into a separate folder.
2. Open the extracted folder.
3. Run the file called *OpenExhibits-Installer.exe.*
4. Follow the instructions to install.

Finally, make sure you have the stand-alone Adobe Flash Player Projector, which can be downloaded at http://www.adobe.com/support/flashplayer/downloads.html. Download the Windows Flash Player 15 Projector; this is a separate executable file, not a browser plug-in. The executable file will be saved to a folder for your projects that you will create next.

Set Up the Software Environment and Download Exhibits

Begin by creating a folder on your local hard drive called *Open Exhibits Project.* Next, copy the Adobe Flash Player Projector file you just downloaded into this new folder. Download the following exhibits from http://openexhibits.org/downloads/exhibits:

- Museum Timeline
- Album Exhibit
- Moon Gigapixel
- Hurricane Sandy Before & After

Save each zipped file to your *Open Exhibits Project* folder. Extract each file to its own folder. Keep the names of the folder the same as each file, this will make it easier.

Next, set up your file associations and trusted location for Adobe Flash Player:

1. Open up your *Open Exhibits Project* folder.
2. Navigate to the folder *\OPEN EXHIBITS\Museum Timeline 1.1\Museum Timeline\bin*.
3. Right-click on the file *Timeline.swf*.
4. Select Open With.
5. Click More Options.
6. Navigate to the Adobe Flash Player Projector within your exhibits folder.

Now your Shockwave Flash (SWF) files will be associated with the Flash Player Projector. Set the trust location for your exhibits folder. This is done to ensure that Adobe Flash Player does not block your SWF files from playing otherwise you will have a black screen:

1. Open your Control panel, in Windows 8, or press the Windows key and type Control Panel to launch the Control panel.
2. Open the Flash Player Settings Manager, by clicking on the Flash icon.
3. Click on the Advanced tab.
4. Scroll down and click the button called Trusted Location Settings…
5. Click Add.
6. Click Add Folder.
7. Navigate to your *Open Exhibits Project* folder.
8. Click OK and Confirm.
9. Close the Flash Player Settings Manager.

You are now ready to customize and run your exhibits.

Customize Your Exhibits

The Open Exhibits framework is designed for developers, author or editor providers, and users. This project will focus on the author/editor to set up your exhibits. If you would like to learn more about the developer side and create more exciting exhibits, go to http://openexhibits.org/support/tutorials and download the developer PDF.

For each exhibit in this project, you will learn how to do the following:

- Determine the correct proportional size for images.
- Create and copy all images to the correct location.
- Configure and customize attributes for the Creative Markup Language (CML) file.
- Identify and edit the proper tags for image location, title, year, and descriptions.

OE Exhibit 1: Museum Timeline

The Museum Timeline is an exhibit that allows users to navigate left or right via a touch display. Each section, called a panel, on the timeline contains two images, a title, the location, a year, and two descriptions. Viewers can touch an information icon to view an additional image with text (figure 5.4).

Image Size, Creation, and Saved Location

Begin with the background image for the exhibit; this will contain the name and logo of your institution along with a title. You are not limited in your creativity and choice of text or background image. Just keep in mind that not all of the background will be visible. Navigate to the *Museum Timeline* folder in your OE projects folder, and from there open the *library/images* folder. Open the file called *timeline-bg.png* in your preferred image manipulation program, such as GIMP 2.8, which is available for free at http://www.gimp.org.

With the image open, you are going to want to either edit the image or create your own. If you are going to create your own background image, make sure that the dimensions are 1920-by-1080 pixels. This will ensure that the image is the proper proportion. If you use a smaller image, it will be stretched beyond its limits and look grainy. If you use larger image, it will scale down and look fine, but it will take longer to load. After you are done creating or editing the image, save it to a location. You can either save it with the same name or create a different name. Saving it with a different name is useful when you want to quick-

Figure 5.4. Open Exhibits Museum Timeline

ly change the background of your timeline exhibit. This type of housekeeping will make managing the exhibit easier.

Next, you will scale, name, and save the images that are used in the exhibit. The timeline uses two images for the each paired-panel entry. Let's call them *image*1 and *image*2, where *image* is the name that briefly describes the image. For example: if you used images from the Museum of Modern Art, you would call the first image **MoMA1** and the second **MoMa2**. Just as the background image was scaled, the images for the panels must be scaled. Both image1 and image2 will be scaled to about 600-by-500 pixels and saved to a location.

Once the background image and all the images for each entry on the timeline are created, copy them to your OE projects folder. The folder will be located at *\OPEN EXHIBITS\Museum Timeline 1.1\Museum Timeline\bin\library\images.* You are not limited to the number of entries for your timeline, but keep in mind that the navigation does not loop to the beginning. Viewers have to swipe back to reach the beginning. If your timeline is very long, if may become tedious for them.

Configure the CML File

The CML file is an XML-based open standard. This allows you to create and share your CML file with others. The file contains the object creation, management, and interaction within a multiuser, multitouch environment. I will be concentrating on the management portion here.

Open the CML file called *Timeline.cml* into a text editor, such as Notepad. The file is located in *\OPEN EXHIBITS\Museum Timeline 1.1\Museum Timeline\bin*.

Look for the node <**StageKit**> and its child node <**Background-Kit**>. Here you will see a <**Image**> node with attributes. Make sure that the *src* is pointing to the proper image file for your background. You can also set whether or not you want it visible by indicating that you want it to be "true" or "false," as shown in the following line of code:

```
<Image id="default-bg" src="library/images/timeline-bg.png" vis-
ible="true"/>
```

Now customize the timeline box and text colors. Look for the following section of code:

```
<RenderKit dataRootTag="museum">
<Renderer>
<TouchContainer width="600" height="890" mouseChil-
dren="true">
<Graphic shape="rectangle" width="600" height="890"
fill="color" color="0xffffff" lineStroke="0" alpha="0.7"/>
```

The text in bold is the node and attribute that will change the color of the timeline entry box. Change the **ffffff** to any desired color; the color codes are in six-digit hexadecimal format. For a general list of color codes, go to http://www.w3schools.com/html/html_colornames.asp.

Next, you are going to edit the colors, font size, font style, location, year, and excerpt. They are modified the same way you changed the color for the entry box, only the node is different. Each one is located at the following nodes:

```
<Text text="{title}" y="520" textAlign="center" color="0x000000" fontSize="30" width="600" font="OpenSansRegular" selectable="false"/>
<Text text="{location}" y="580" textAlign="center" color="0x303030" fontSize="30" width="600" font="OpenSansRegular" selectable="false"/>
<Text text="{year}" y="620" textAlign="center" color="0x000000" fontSize="70" width="600" font="OpenSansRegular" selectable="false"/>
<Text text="{excerpt}" x="20" y="730" selectable="false" color="0x000000" fontSize="20" alpha="0.6" wordWrap="true" multiline="true" width="540" height="300" font="OpenSansRegular"/>
```

Each node has an open and close angle bracket tag. So for the title, it would contain everything between **<Text text="{title}" ... />**. Every node has the following attributes that you can edit:

- Color: This is the six-digit hexadecimal color code.
- Font size: The size of the text.
- Font: The font style; you can choose Regular, Bold, or Italic. The format is OpenSans[font style], for example, bold is **OpenSans-Bold**.

Other attributes include x,y, textAlign (center, left, right), and width. Feel free to experiment and change some of them, you may end up with some interesting results! The CML is designed so you virtually cannot break the code. If the changed attribute results in an undesirable look, simply undo the changes.

Finally, make changes to the second panel called “museum-text.” Follow the instruction for the previous nodes:

```
<Text id="txt1" text="{museum-text}" x="50" y="540" width="500" height="860" color="0xffffff" wordWrap="true" multiline="true" fontSize="20" font="OpenSansRegular"/>
```

Panel Data Structure

Each panel contains two images, title, year, location, and two descriptions. The structure is as follows:

```
<museum>
<button-dispatch>down:smithsonian</button-dispatch>
<panel-id>smithsonian</panel-id>
<imagepath>library/images/smithsonian.jpg</imagepath>
<imagepath-2>library/images/smithsonian2.jpg</imagepath-2>
<title>Smithsonian Institution</title>
<location>Washington D.C.</location>
<year>1846</year>
<excerpt>The Smithsonian Institution, established in 1846 "for the increase and diffusion of knowledge", is a group of museums and research centers administered by the United States government.</excerpt>
<museum-text>Termed "the nation's attic" for its eclectic holdings of 137 million items, the Institution's Washington, D.C. nucleus of nineteen museums, nine research centers, and zoo—many of them historical or architectural landmarks—is the largest such complex in the world. Additional facilities are located in Arizona, Maryland, New York City, Virginia, Panama and elsewhere, and 168 other museums are Smithsonian affiliates.</museum-text>
</museum>
```

There are no attributes in the data structure; you will assign IDs, set image paths, and set text. Each node that you edit is listed below in the order as they appear. Make your changes inside the angle brackets:

- **<button-dispatch>…</button-dispatch>**: This is a unique ID that you create for the button. The format is **down:** *name*, where *name* is the unique ID.
- **<panel-id>…</panel-id>**: This should be the same as the unique ID without the preceding **down:**.
- **<imagepath>…</imagepath>**: This is the location of *image*1, the main panel. Its format is similar to *src*, which was used for the background: *library/images/image1.jpg*
- **<imagepath-2>…</imagepath-2>**: This is the location of *image*2, the second panel.
- **<title>…</title>**: Title for first panel of the entry.
- **<location>…</location>**: Location for first panel of the entry.
- **<year>…</year>**: Year for first panel of the entry.

- **<excerpt>...</excerpt>**: The description for first panel of the entry.
- **<museum-text>...</museum-text>**: The description for second panel of the entry.

When all the changes are made to the CML file, save the file and launch the Museum Timeline Exhibit. To launch the exhibit, go to *OPEN EXHIBITS\Museum Timeline 1.1\Museum Timeline\bin* and double-click on *Timeline.exe.* Check to make sure the timeline is working correctly.

OE Exhibit 2: Album Exhibit

The Album Exhibit, which is called Photo Album Viewer, allows you to display both images and videos along with a brief description for each. Users can scroll in a left or right direction to view full-screen images or video. An information icon is added to each image or video. This allows users to see a brief description, which is overlaid on the image or video (figure 5.5). For this section of the project, I will refer to the Album Exhibit as Photo Album Viewer.

Now that you are familiar with setting up your first OE, the Timeline Exhibit, setting up the next exhibit will be easier and will follow a similar pattern.

Image/Video Size, Creation, and Saved Location

The Photo Album Viewer does not use a background image. You will only use images and video that is displayed one at a time. Begin by ensuring that your images are the proper dimensions. As with all the exhibits, the dimensions should be as close to 1920-by-1080 pixels as possible.

Any video that is used should also be proportional to the dimensions size. Any smaller dimensions will be stretched by the viewer. Images should be in JPG format and videos in MP4 format, this will ensure proper viewing and playback.

The naming of both images and videos is not restricted. Keep in mind that a good naming schema will make it easier to manage the exhibit. For example, if your exhibit is on nineteenth-century Women in Science and your image is of Marie Curie, one way to name the image is

Figure 5.5. Open Exhibits Album Exhibit

by using an abbreviation for the exhibit title, such as 19thwos, then use the first initial and last name. Separate the title and name with an underscore. So nineteenth-century Woman of Science with an image of Marie Curie would be 19thwos_mcurie. Try to avoid using long file names, spaces, and uncommon naming characters, such as an exclamation point, the at symbol, a dollar sign, or percent sign.

Once all of your images and videos have been created, copy them to your OE projects folder. The folder will be located at *\OPEN EXHIBITS\Photo Album Viewer\bin\assets.* You are not limited to the number of images or videos for your album. Unlike the Timeline Exhibit, the navigation can be toggled to loop from front to back and vice versa. This will allow you to add several images without worrying about making the exhibit tedious to navigate.

Configure the CML File

Open the CML file called *PhotoAlbumViewer.cml* into a text editor. The file is located in *\OPEN EXHIBITS\Photo Album Viewer.* Begin by setting the viewer for loop and swipe navigation. Look for the following nodes, both the front and back:

```
<Album id="front" loop="true" horizontal="true" applyMask="true" margin="8" visible="true" targetParent="false" mouseChildren="true" clusterBubbling="true" dragGesture="n-drag-album">
<Album id="back" alpha=".5" loop="false" applyMask="true" horizontal="true" margin="8" visible="false" targetParent="false" dragGesture="n-drag-album">
```

If the exhibit is going to be set for loop navigation, that is, when the user reaches the end, it simply starts with the first image and vice versa, set the following attribute to true—**horizontal="true"**—this should be set for both front and back navigation.

Next, set the reset time for the information icon. This setting is in seconds, and it is the time the information is displayed before returning to the image or video. Enter the number of seconds in the attribute **resetTime="600"**. The attribute can be found at the following node:

```
<PhotoAlbumViewer id="av" x="0" y="0" rotation="0" autoTextLayout="false" linkAlbums="true" gestureReleaseInertia="true" resetTime="600" videoScrollAction="stop" playOnComplete="true">
```

Once the viewer settings are set, the image and video locations, names, and descriptions have to be set. Both the image and video nodes are separate from the description nodes.

Begin with the image node, which has the following format:

```
<Image name="Space Station Over Earth" src="image4.jpg" width="1920" height="1080"/>
```

The parts of this node that you can set include:

- name: This is the descriptive name for the image, it is used to help make it easier to find the node in your CML file.
- src: This is the location of the file, the default location is the *assets* folder. Use the file name plus the file extension.
- width and height: These two attributes will set the image display dimensions—use caution if changing these attributes. The viewer is designed to be shown in full-screen mode.

The video node uses the same types of attributes; the only exception is that the name attribute is not present. Look for the video node, which has the following format:

```
<TouchContainer class="player" width="1920" height="1080"
mouseChildren="false" disableNativeTransform="true">
<Video src="NASA.mp4" width="1920" height="1080"/>
<Graphic shape="triangle" height="200" rotation="90"
x="1060" y="440" alpha=".5"/>
<GestureList>
<Gesture ref="n-tap" gestureOn="true"/>
</GestureList>
</TouchContainer>
```

You can set the src, width, and height attributes.

Finally, the descriptions for each image and video must be set. Each node contains two child nodes: title and description. Each entry is matched to the image or video order, so the first image/video node is linked to the first text node. Below is the format:

```
<TouchContainer width="1920" height="1080">
<Graphic shape="rectangle" color="0x000000" width="1920"
height="1080"/>
<Text class="title" y="220" text="Space Station Over Earth"
width="1920" fontSize="50" textAlign="center" col-
or="0xFFFFFF"/>
<Text class="description" y="300" text="NASA" width="1920"
color="0xFFFFFF" fontSize="30" textAlign="center"/>
</TouchContainer>
```

The two child nodes for the title and description are as follows:

- **<Text class="title".../>**
- **<Text class="description".../>**

Each node contains the following attributes:

- text: The text displayed for either the title or description.
- fontSize: The size of the text to be displayed.

- width: This is the character limit that will be displayed, and it should not be changed unless your image width was changed.
- color: The color of the displayed text.

Once all of the images and videos are created and saved, viewer attributes set, image and videos source attributes set, and the descriptions set, save the CML file. The exhibit is ready to be tested and to go live. To run the exhibit, execute the SWF file called *PhotoAlbumViewer*. It is located in the folder *\OPEN EXHIBITS\Photo Album Viewer/bin*.

OE Exhibit 3: Moon Gigapixel

The Moon Gigapixel Exhibit uses normal images as well as one panoramic image, which is scalable. What makes the exhibit unique is that it uses high-definition view to render the panoramic image. This enables the exhibit to have a large image that users can zoom into and out of. The zooming of such large images is fluid and users don't have to wait for the image to download and reform.

The exhibit is laid out with two regions. The area on the left is for general images that can be viewed by scrolling up and down. It is not designed to zoom in or out, nor does it list more details of the images when clicked on. The region center to right is more interactive. The user can pan and zoom the panoramic image. There are also hotspots where a user can view a description and an additional image when the spot is selected (figure 5.6).

In order to use the Moon Gigapixel Exhibit, a panoramic image must be created. Instructions on how to create a high-definition view image were detailed in chapter 3 in the section "Microsoft Research Image Composite Editor." Ensure that the file name you save is called *moon* and save it in a separate folder.

Once the high-definition view is created, rename and copy all of the necessary files to the Moon Gigapixel Exhibit. The files will consist of one folder containing all the tile images with the name you chose to save and four files with the following names, where *yourname* is the save name:

- HDViewSL.xap

Figure 5.6. Open Exhibits Moon Gigapixel

- *Yourname*.html
- *Yourname*.xml
- *Yourname*_hdv.xml

Make sure to rename *yourname* folder to *moon* and the files with *yourname* to *moon*. So the file *yourname*.html will be renamed *moon.html*, *yourname*.xml to *moon.xml*, and *yourname*_hdv.xml to *moon_hdv.xml*.

Open the folder *\OPEN EXHIBITS\Gigapixel Moon* and navigate to the moon folder. It is located under *library/moon*. Copy and replace all of the following files and folders—these should be the files you just created when you made your panoramic image in Microsoft Research Image Composite Editor:

- *moon_files* (folder)
- *HDViewSL.xap*
- *moon.html*
- *moon.xml*
- *moon_hdv.xml*

After the high-definition view image is copied, edit the CML files. The Moon Gigapixel Exhibit uses several CML files:

- base.cml: This file contains the static-image names of the right region. It also sets the title name and the custom icon for the exhibit.
- hotspot.cml: This file sets the custom info-icon.
- Six CML files for each hotspot:

    a. *bear-mtn.cml*
    b. *east-massif.cml*
    c. *family-mtn.cml*
    d. *north-massif.cml*
    e. *south-massif.cml*
    f. *sculptured-hills.cml*

Begin with the *base.cml* file. Its location is in the folder *\OPEN EXHIBITS\Gigapixel Moon\library\cml.* Look at the following code:

```
<!-- Albums -->
<RenderKit>
<Renderer dataRootTag="album" dataPath="locations/index.cml">
<Include src="library/cml/renderers/album.cml" />
</Renderer>
</RenderKit>
<Container class="block">
<Graphic x="0" y="0" shape="rectangle" width="400" height="1080"
fill="color" color="0x000000" lineStroke="0" alpha="0.7" />
<Image src="library/images/shuttle-icon.png" x="20" y="20"
width="40"/>
<Text text="Apollo 17 Moon Landing" color="0xffffff" x="70" y="30"
fontSize="27" width="500" multiline="true" wordWrap="true" />
</Container>
<Album x="20" y="100" margin="0" horizontal="false" height="1080"
backgroundAlpha="0">
<Image src="library/images/1.jpg" width="360"/>
<Image src="library/images/2.jpg" width="360" />
<Image src="library/images/3.jpg" width="360" />
<Image src="library/images/4.jpg" width="360"/>
<Image src="library/images/5.jpg" width="360"/>
<Image src="library/images/6.jpg" width="360"/>
<Image src="library/images/7.jpg" width="360"/>
<Image src="library/images/8.jpg" width="360"/>
```

```
<Image src="library/images/9.jpg" width="360"/>
<Image src="library/images/10.jpg" width="360"/>
<Image src="library/images/11.jpg" width="360"/>
<Image src="library/images/12.jpg" width="360"/>
<Image src="library/images/13.jpg" width="360"/>
</Album>
```

The icon default name is called *shuttle-icon.png*. Here is where you have the opportunity to change the name of the icon to the PNG file that you would like to use. This can be your library's logo, or it can be a logo that represents the exhibit you are creating. For example, if you were doing an exhibit on International Woman's Day, you might choose to use their official iconic purple logo. Then make sure to copy the file to the images folder located at *\OPEN EXHIBITS\Gigapixel Moon\library\images*. Ensure that the icon is a proper size. There is no exact size or limitation. But it is best to use an image that is not larger than 150-by-150 pixels. Anything larger may not be proportional to the entire layout and will look oddly out of place.

Next, add the images for the left region—these images are added to complement the exhibit. The right region will have images arranged in a filmstrip-type fashion that users can scroll up and down. Copy them to the images folder *\OPEN EXHIBITS\Gigapixel Moon\library\images*. Make sure that the images are of equal proportion in height and width. Any images that are not of proper proportion will be skewed when displayed. The default image size is 460-by-460 pixels. Limit your images to approximately that size.

There is no limit to the number of images. It is important to remember that users will scroll up and down to view images, so keep the number of images to a reasonable amount. Each image is displayed in the order that it is listed in the CML file.

A template tag for each image is listed as such: **<Image src="library/images/13.jpg" width="360"/>**. The image name should correspond with the image you want to display. Changing the width attribute within the tag will alter the size of that image. Make sure the width attribute is consistent for all the images listed. Changing one width attribute will not apply to all images.

Next, edit the *hospot.cml* file—it is located in the folder *\OPEN EXHIBITS\Gigapixel Moon\library\cml\renderers*. In this file, the info-icon will be changed. Look for the following tag: **<Image id="graphic"**

src="library/images/moon-info.png"/>. It is listed three times in the file. The file *moon-info.png* can be changed to a different information icon of your choosing. If you choose not to use the default black-and-white icon, change the entry *moon-info.png* to the file you want to use. Make sure to copy the icon file to the images folder. Also make sure the icon image is of the proper size. The default icon is 50-by-51 pixels.

Finally, edit the hotspot CML. There are six CML files. The hotspots are of a fixed number:

- *sculptured-hills.cml*
- *east-mtn.cml*
- *bear-mtn.cml*
- *south massif.cml*
- *family-mtn.cml*
- *north-massif.cml*

Each file is located at *\OPEN EXHIBITS\Gigapixel Moon\locations*. Each hotspot is listed in order. The order cannot be changed, so ensure that the layout and images you want to display are in the proper order. Do not rename any of these six CML files. Do not remove any of these CML files. Doing so will not display that hotspot correctly and will result in empty areas.

Begin by editing the first CML, *sculptured-hills.cml*. The other CML files will be edited in the same manner. The following areas will be edited:

```
<hotspot>
<scene-x>1400</scene-x>
<scene-y>265</scene-y>
<album-id>sculptured-hills-album</album-id>
<id>sculptured-hills</id>
<location-title>Sculptured Hills</location-title>
<button-x>380</button-x>
<button-y>10</button-y>
</hotspot>
<album>
<id>sculptured-hills-album</id>
<panel-path>locations/sculptured-hills.cml</panel-path>
<title-en>Sculptured Hills</title-en>
</album>
```

<panel>
<media-source>locations/media/sculptured-hills.jpg</media-source>
<description-en>
The Sculptured Hills are underlain by material that may be different from the material beneath the massifs. Its different appearance is largely the result of its different topographic expression. The Sculptured Hills unit forms several closely spaced and rounded hills.
</description-en>
</panel>

The parent tag **<hotspot>** contains the title heading that will be displayed on the high-definition view image. Each hotspot is a section that is placed on your panoramic high-definition view image. You can edit the title that appears over the hotspot. For example, suppose the high-definition view image is of the White House and your hotspot is of the West Wing. The title above the hotspot that patrons will see can be edited to say something like "WH West Wing."

To edit the title heading, you would edit its contents in the following child tag: **<location-title>Sculptured Hills</location-title>**. Next look for the **<album>** parent tag. This tag contains the heading for the inside title when a user clicks on the info-icon. Edit the following: **<title-en>Sculptured Hills</title-en>**. The title does not have to match the title of the hotspot tag.

Lastly, the image names and description tags can be edited. Look for the **<panel>** tag; it contains the entries for the image and description. Within the tag is **<media-source>locations/media/sculptured-hills.jpg</media-source>**. Change the name of the image that will be used for the info hotspot. Further down, the child tag **<description-en> … </description-en>**contains the detail information about the image.

After all of the CML files have been edited, the last step is to copy the hotspot panel images to the media folder. Its location is *\OPEN EXHIBITS\Gigapixel Moon\locations\media*. It is best to keep the images to no more than 1024-by-1024 pixels in size. Once the files are copied, the exhibit can be started and tested for accuracy. Locate the file *GigapixelMoonLanding.exe* in the folder *\OPEN EXHIBITS\Gigapixel Moon* and run it.

OE Exhibit 4: Hurricane Sandy Before & After

This last Open Exhibits project is quite unique. It is included in the project list not only because it is different from the previous Open Exhibits projects, but because it is also extremely easy to set up. This OE uses images and information text as did the other OEs in this project list. The exciting difference is that it uses two images to create a before-and-after effect (figure 5.7). Users are able to pan and zoom on an image. Then, with a movable overlay, they can see the before or after effects of an image. This type of exhibit would be quite useful for a digital collection that has before and after images of town, cities, or interior buildings. The important thing to remember is that images must be in exact proportion to each other for the effect to work.

Before creating this exhibit, make sure that all images are properly labeled with a notation scheme for before and after. An example of this is attaching an extension to the name such as "_before" or "_after". Another example is to use letters such as "a" and "b", where "a" would stand for after and "b" would stand for before. Try to avoid using numbers. This can often confuse those who will maintain the exhibit collection afterward. When all the before and after images are properly labeled, save them to a separate folder so they can be copied later.

Figure 5.7. Open Exhibits Hurricane Sandy Before & After

The Hurricane Sandy Before & After Exhibit structure is very similar to that of the previous OE Moon Gigapixel. Each set of before and after images has one CML file associated with the set. The images are all located in one folder, called the *assets* folder. All image sets are added to one CML file for the exhibit.

Begin by editing the first image-set CML file. Use the CML file called *Atlantic_City_1.cml* as a template. It is located in the CML folder *\OPEN EXHIBITS\Hurricane Sandy Before-After\library\cml*. Look for the following tags:

```
<TouchContainer id="t" class="base_img" dimensionsTo="image" mouseChildren="false">
<Image id="image" x="0" y="0" src="library/assets/Atlantic_City_1_b.jpg"/>
</TouchContainer>
<MaskContainer maskShape="rectangle" maskWidth="250" maskHeight="200" maskBorderColor="0xff0000" maskBorderStroke="4" maskBorderAlpha="0.75" mouseChildren="false">
<Image id="image2" x="0" y="0" visible="false" src="library/assets/Atlantic_City_1_a.jpg"/>
<GestureList>
<Gesture ref="n-double_tap" gestureOn="true"/>
<Gesture ref="n-drag" gestureOn="true"/>
<Gesture ref="n-scale" gestureOn="true"/>
<Gesture ref="n-rotate" gestureOn="true"/>
</GestureList>
</MaskContainer>
<TouchContainer id="img1-info" class="info_container" visible="false" targetParent="true" mouseChildren="false">
<Graphic id="info-bg" class="info_bg" shape="rectangle"/>
<Text class="info_title" selectable="false" border="false" textSize="38" text="Atlantic City, New Jersey"/>
<Text id="description" class="info_description" selectable="false" border="false" text="Before and after Hurricane Sandy, 2012."/>
</TouchContainer>
```

The tag **<Image id="image" x="0" y="0" src="library/assets/Atlantic_City_1_b.jpg"/>** contains the before image. Replace **Atlantic_City_1_b** with the before image of the first set.

Next look for the tag **<Image id="image2" x="0" y="0" visible="false" src="library/assets/Atlantic_City_1_a.jpg"/>**. This contains the after image. Replace **Atlantic_City_1_a** with the after image of the set.

Next locate the tag **<TouchContainer id="img1-info" class="info_container" visible="false" targetParent="true" mouseChildren="false">**. This tag contains the title and description that will be displayed when the user touches the info-icon.

The tag **<Text class="info_title" selectable="false" border="false" textSize="38" text="Atlantic City, New Jersey"/>** holds the title. You can edit the attribute **text="Atlantic City, New Jersey"**. You would enter the desired title between the double quotation marks.

Finally, locate the tag **<Text id="description" class="info_description" selectable="false" border="false" text="Before and after Hurricane Sandy, 2012."/>**. This tag contains the brief description for the image set. Edit the attribute **text="Before and after Hurricane Sandy, 2012."** Once the CML is edited, save it with the same name as the image set. For example, if the image set has the files *statepark_before.jpg* and *statepark_after.jpg*, name the CML file *statepark*. Create and edit a CML file for each image set.

After all the CML files are created, the main CML file must be edited. Locate the CML file called *HurricaneSandy*. It is located in the folder *\OPEN EXHIBITS\Hurricane Sandy Before-After\library\cml*. The default file will contain the following:

```
<CollectionViewer id="collection" layout="layout0" amountToShow="3" autoShuffle="true" mouseChildren="true" animateIn="true">
<Include cml="library/cml/Atlantic_City_1.cml"/>
<Include cml="library/cml/Brick_Township_1.cml"/>
<Include cml="library/cml/Gillians_Island_Water_Park_1.cml"/>
<Include cml="library/cml/Gillians_Wonderland_Pier_1.cml"/>
<Include cml="library/cml/Longport_Coastline_1.cml"/>
<Include cml="library/cml/Longport_Coastline_2.cml"/>
<Include cml="library/cml/Longport_Coastline_3.cml"/>
<Include cml="library/cml/Mantoloking_1.cml"/>
```

```
<Include cml="library/cml/Mantoloking_2.cml"/>
<Include cml="library/cml/Near_Brielle_1.cml"/>
<Include cml="library/cml/Ocean_City_1.cml"/>
<Include cml="library/cml/Ocean_City_coast_1.cml"/>
<Include cml="library/cml/Playlands_Castaway_Cove_1.cml"/>
</CollectionViewer>
```

All the **<include cml>** tags will be replaced with the names of the image sets for the exhibit. Start with the following tag: **<Include cml="library/cml/Atlantic_City_1.cml"/>**. Use this template for all the image sets. Replace **Atlantic_City_1** with the name of the first image set CML file. Continue adding all the image set CML files created previously. After each CML tag is added, save the *HurricaneSandy* CML file.

Finally, copy all of the image files to the *assets* folder located at *\OPEN EXHIBITS\Hurricane Sandy Before-After\library\assets.* Run and test the exhibit for accuracy. The executable *Hurricane Sandy Before-After.exe* is located in the folder *Hurricane Sandy Before-After* under *\OPEN EXHIBITS\Hurricane Sandy Before-After.* The exhibit only displays three images at one time. If a user closes an image, a random image from the sets will be displayed. Three images are always displayed at any given time.

Open Exhibits is a great framework not only for developing original exhibits, but it is also highly scalable. It is designed so that digital exhibit creators can take an existing exhibit that may seem specifically designed for a particular exhibit and make it their own. With a little bit of tweaking, any OE can be transformed from the default exhibit to an exhibit that is completely customized to your projects.

HOW TO CREATE 3D OBJECTS AND ADD THEM TO ONLINE EXHIBITS

123D Catch is a free application that can create 3D objects without the need for expensive capturing devices. The Smithsonian Institute has an online exhibit called Smithsonian X 3D at http://3d.si.edu/. This exciting exhibit has a collection of objects that are rendered in 3D that users can view online. The exhibit is powered by Autodesk, an industry leader in computer-aided design (CAD) software. Autodesk has evolved to support industries that include visual special effects, animation, and game development. This project will use one of Autodesk's applications called 123D Catch.

In this project, you will learn the following:

- What 123D Catch is.
- The difference between each version of 123D Catch.
- How to install 123D Catch on your mobile device.
- How to best capture an object.
- How to upload a 3D object online.
- How to add the 3D object to your online exhibit.

So what is 123D Catch? It is an application that uses ordinary digital photos to create a 3D-rendered object for viewing. Images can either be captured in real time or may be already existing images. The program seamlessly creates the 3D object; there is no need to manipulate the images. The player allows users to rotate the object a full 360 degrees. The 3D object can be embedded into an online exhibit with ease.

123D Catch Versions

123D Catch is available for both iOS and Android devices. It is also available for Windows PC as well as in an online version. The iOS and Android versions allow you to capture images with the device's camera. Both the Windows and online versions do not incorporate a camera, instead images are imported into the system to create a 3D object. For this project, you are going to use the mobile versions. You can choose between the iOS or Android version, as both are essentially the same in functionality.

Installation and Account Creation

Begin by downloading either the iOS or Android version of 123D Catch. The iOS version can be downloaded from the Apple App Store at https://itunes.apple.com/us/app/123d-catch/id513913018?ls=1&mt=8; the Android version can be obtained from the Google Play Store at https://play.google.com/store/apps/details?id=com.autodesk.Catch. Install either version as you would normally install a mobile app.

Once you have installed the app, you will need to create an account or link an existing Facebook account to create 3D objects. 123D Catch uses special online servers to process your images, therefore, you will not be able to create 3D objects without an account. In addition, the app requires an Internet connection to upload the images to the servers. It is best that you create or link a Facebook account before starting a project.

To create or link a Facebook account, go to https://www.123dapp.com/gopremium and sign up for a free account. You will enter a valid e-mail address and create a password. If you are using the mobile version to sign up, click on the context menu and select Sign in / join. If you want to link your Facebook account, use your Facebook e-mail address or mobile phone and password to link to 123D Catch. 123D Catch also allows you to link the following accounts:

- Google
- Twitter
- Yahoo!
- LinkedIn
- Microsoft

How to Capture an Object for 3D

123D Catch uses a series of overlapping images to create a 3D object. Start by placing the item on a flat surface, such as a table. For best results, use a plain surface that is not too reflective. The application has a difficult time processing shiny surfaces. For this project, you will want to start with something simple, such as a coffee cup or small figurine. Make sure that the object is not shiny or reflective.

Begin by taking a series of overlapping pictures. 123D Catch suggests that you imagine your camera is attached to the object with an invisible string. Walking around the object, take plenty of overlapping images, make sure the frame is filled with the entire item. As you walk around taking pictures, take them at varying heights. Do a couple of complete walk arounds from above and below. 123D Catch recommends twenty to forty images in total. Take your time when capturing images, do not rush.

For best results, make sure the lighting is even around the object. Too much or not enough makes it difficult for 123D Catch to render the object in 3D. Ensure that there is contrast between the surface and the item. Capturing a white object on a white surface will result in a poor 3D object. The item must not be shiny or have reflective surfaces. If you are going to create a 3D object with a person as your model, you will want to make sure the person remains still. Try not to have the person pose in difficult positions; the model should be natural and comfortable.

Once you are done capturing the images, it is time to review them. Review each image and delete any that have one or more of the following:

- Image frame: Make sure the entire object is in the shot.
- Blurred image: 123D Catch will get confused.
- Lighting: Poorly lit images will not render well.
- Shiny or reflective: These images cannot be processed.
- Moving objects: This applies to live subjects.

After you have reviewed all the images and have chosen the best ones, upload them for processing. Upload begins immediately after you click Done. Depending on the number of images you have taken, the process can take some time. You should make sure your device has plenty of power. If your device goes into sleep mode, do not worry; the process will resume once it wakes up. Also, if you do not have an active Internet connection, the images will be stored for uploading later, once your device is online.

Review and Share Your 3D Object

Now that you have created the 3D object, you are ready to review and share it. Make sure you review the object first. If you are not happy with the results, you can delete it and start over. Do not get frustrated if you do not get great results at first. 123D Catch is a great tool, but it does take practice and patience. 123D Catch will give you a push notification when it is ready for review.

Sharing your project is done in three easy steps.

- Keep: Review the capture and click Next to keep.
- Frame: Zoom in or out, rotate, or flip the capture to how you want it to look in the gallery.
- Sharing: Select share, add a title, description, or tags, and share.

Once you have shared the project, you can go to http://www.123dapp.com/catch and use several tools to clean up your capture. You can also download and use the Windows version of 123D Catch to edit your capture.

How to Add 3D Objects to Your Online Exhibit

The final step is to add the 3D capture to your online exhibit. Autodesk, the maker of 123D Catch, makes it very easy for you to embed the 3D object into your online exhibit. Embedding your capture is done just like other sites that share content, such as YouTube and Vimeo. Your capture is embedded using iframes.

First, log in to your account at http://www.123dapp.com/catch. Once there, click on the ME icon and from the dropdown menu, select Models. Now, select the model you want to embed and follow these steps:

1. Selecting it will take you to the view of the model.
2. Click on the embed icon (chain link).
3. That will bring up a box with the embed code.
4. Select the size of the embed model: 338 × 390px, 495 × 555px, or 635 × 730px.
5. Click on the embed code to highlight it and copy it to your clipboard.

Here is an example of the embed iframe code you will copy:

```
<iframe id='embed3DViewer' src='http://www.123dapp.com/fullpreview/embedViewer?assetId=2908052&size=small' scrolling='no' style='border:none; width: 338px; height: 390px'></iframe>
```

Note, you can modify the style with CSS code, and you can also change the width and height of the iframe. The assetId is the unique identifier associated with your 3D model.

Now add the embed code to your online exhibit. Here is a basic working HTML example using an embedded 3D object. The embed code is in bold:

```
<!DOCTYPE html>
<html>
<head><title>My 3D Object</title></head>
<body>
<h1>Fisheye / Macro Lens for iPhone 4s</h1>
<iframe id='embed3DViewer'>
src='http://www.123dapp.com/fullpreview/embedView-
er?assetId=2908052&size=small'
scrolling='no' style='border:none; width: 338px; height: 390px'
target="_blank">
</iframe>
</body>
</html>
```

There is no need for costly processing hardware; it is done with the application's online servers. The application allows you to capture images using a mobile device, such as an iPad or smartphone. You can also upload images that you have taken with a regular digital camera. You are no longer bound to the limitations of expensive 3D laser scanning equipment to capture 3D objects. With the added benefit of mobile devices, you can easily capture objects that may otherwise be hard to obtain. Imagine being able to capture rare objects or books from your special collections without having to be trained in handling them. You can simply have the curator set up the item, then you can walk around the object and capture images. The item never leaves its place of origin. Now, with this free application and 123D Catch servers, you can create and link exciting new 3D objects to your digital exhibit. Users will be surrounded by a wonderful 3D world of objects from your collections.

6

TIPS AND TRICKS

The projects in this book are designed for both the beginner and the more advanced user. Each project can evolve to an advanced level. It doesn't matter whether you are just starting out developing digital exhibits or you are on your way to mastery, there are some best practices that are useful to know. The best practices covered in this chapter will include suggestions for both creating and maintaining a digital exhibit.

EVERYTHING IS IMPOSSIBLE UNTIL SOMEONE DOES IT

Librarians often find themselves asking "Is it possible?" or, "Can we do this?" They not only ask it among other librarians, but they also ask information technology people as well. My response is always, "Anything is possible." The reason why I tell librarians this is because their "can we" is often preceded with an "I saw this at . . ." If you see something another library or museum has created, then the chance of re-creating is definitely within the realm of possibility. Sure, some digital exhibits may go beyond your capabilities, but that should not discourage you from trying to create one. It might require you to give up some of the advanced features or create an exhibit on a smaller scale, but you may find that some of your ideas made the original better. Don't be afraid to try.

GET INVOLVED WITH THE DIGITAL COMMUNITY

Now that you know that everything is impossible until someone does it and creating it is not beyond your reach, it is important to get involved in the digital community. Be sure to connect with forums and listservs, and go beyond the library and museum forums and listservs. Do not be afraid to reach out to the developer's world. Much of the *innovation* you will use in your digital exhibits will come from programmers and developers. It is important to know that they enjoy getting their ideas and projects out there. They also enjoy helping those who may have trouble implementing a script or program.

However, participation in the community is expected to be a two-way street. If you happen to create a great plug-in for a digital framework, such as Omeka, share it with the larger community. Do not be discouraged if you feel it is not as great as some of the others. It is a great way to show that you are part of the community.

Helping others by sharing your success and failures is also a great way to get involved. The more you share, the more you will find others willing to help. Some forums do not even allow you to ask questions until you have answered a few.

HAVE A BACKUP PLAN

One thing you will never have to worry about with a print exhibit is content disappearing. Sure, you may have to replace it due to vandalism or the print falling off the mount, but staring at a blank screen or the infamous Windows "Blue Screen of Death" will never happen. You may find, however, that digital exhibits do occasionally fall victim to such mishaps.

It is best to have a backup plan, and not the kind that information technology personnel use when a server goes down. You won't need to cut over to some backup server, as if the digital exhibit was critical to the library's daily operations. Nonetheless, it is important to have a plan for when the digital exhibit stops working.

It is wise to ensure that the person who created the exhibit is not the only one who knows what do in case of an emergency. Even something as simple as restarting a computer or display might go beyond the basic knowledge of some. Make sure that at least one other person knows how to restart the exhibit. If you are putting the exhibit in a specific area, for example, the circulation desk of your library, then it is best for those working the desk to know how to restart a system. Write detailed instructions with images so those working behind the desk can easily restart it. One of the worst visuals a digital exhibit can have is the "Out of Order" sign. This is not only unappealing, but it also gives the impression that a system is truly not working. Oftentimes the system simply needs to be restarted or turned on.

With your backup plan, make sure that your staff know how the digital exhibit works. This will help them report or restart a system. For example, staff might notice that the digital exhibit is displaying a log-in screen because a user accidentally logged off the machine. Because the staff knows that the system does not require a log in to run the exhibit, they will know something is wrong and either restart or report it. In addition to the ill-fated "Out of Order" sign, there is the error pop-up or log-in message: Make sure that staff know the signs.

BACKUP, BACKUP, BACKUP

This type of backup is not the same as your backup plan for when the system is down. This involves preserving the files that are needed to run the digital exhibit. It is important to have a safe copy of not only the digital content, but also the files that run the exhibit.

The option for backing up your digital exhibit is to create an image of the system that is running your software. This includes all the content, special software, and operating systems. Imaging consists of creating an exact copy of a computer's hard drive. The image can then be copied to another computer that has the same exact hardware. The benefit is that a duplicate system can be up and running within a matter of minutes. It is not necessary to configure the system. One can simply swap the dead computer with a duplicate. If your library has an information technology department, they should be able to help you with imaging your system. Note that if your project is running on a self-hosted system, such as an Omeka project, imaging your system is not necessary. The hosting company does backups for you.

Those in the information technology community have long been familiar with the commercial cloning software by Symantec called Norton Ghost. Symantec has since discontinued Ghost and revamped into an all new cloning and backup software called Symantec System Recovery. It contains much of the greatness of the original Ghost software. New robust features make it even better. Another industry leader that is worth looking into for cloning is Acronis True Image. Acronis has been on the top of the list for information technology users because the software's features for cloning are superb. The developers at Acronis know cloning from an information technology standpoint.

Both Symantec System Recovery and Acronis True Image come at a price. Librarians are always looking for high-quality free alternatives. For those who do not want to pay the high cost of commercial software, there are great free alternatives. Paragon Backup and Recovery (Advanced) Free is an excellent solution for creating backup images. Another free backup software solution is Drive Image XML. This program allows you to create images as well as recover them. One other free cloning program worth noting is Clonezilla. Although the interface may seem difficult to use, those in information technology who have used Norton's Ghost will take to Clonezilla with ease. If you have information technology support, be sure to ask for their assistance.

Make sure to back up your digital content to several formats. Having just one copy on an external hard drive is not enough. Make copies on the system itself. Burn a copy to a DVD. Create copies on an external hard drive. If your library has a server that holds shared files, use that as a backup. Those systems often have backups in place. This will help to ensure that you have double protection.

In addition to the content files, make sure you include all the needed configuration files. Projects such as the Open Exhibits projects in chapter 5 use a lot of specific configuration files. It is a best practice to keep copies of those files. This will help minimize the need to configure the digital exhibit if you ever have to bring up a new machine.

Backing up any license keys and specific software is also recommended. It is much easier to reinstall an application from a copied file than to have to search for it on the Internet. Some software vendors do not provide links on their website for download. The private links are sent electronically. Keep copies of any electronic paperwork that a vendor might give you.

TO UPDATE OR NOT TO UPDATE?

The Windows operating system is notorious for needing updates. Some updates are minor, while others are much more important. When using a computer for normal use, it is important to keep your computer updated. Updates help to close any vulnerable security holes in an operating system.

Computers used for digital exhibits do not always need updates. In fact, some updates may actually stop the exhibit from working properly. Many systems such as digital signage and public document scanners disable automatic updates. The reason is that some ports that the program might use get closed with certain updates. Some graphics might not work correctly, or a third-party application that the system depends on might not work correctly.

If your digital exhibit does not require the use of the Internet or is not connected to a network, then it is best not to run updates. Updates should only be installed if the software developer insists on it. This practice does not leave the system vulnerable to online attacks.

Additionally, if the system requires an Internet connection, make sure to test the system after any updates. Windows has a system restore feature that will undo any system or updates based on a specific date. This restore does not affect any documents. In Windows 7, a system restore can be done as follows.

- Navigate to the **Start > All Programs > Accessories > System Tools** program group.
- Click on the System Restore program icon.
- Click Next on the *Restore system files and settings* window.
- Choose the restore point you want to use.
- Click Next.
- Click Finish on the *Confirm your restore point window to begin the System Restore.*
- Click Yes to the *Once started, System Restore cannot be interrupted. Do you want to continue?* dialog box.
- System Restore will restore Windows 7 to the state that was recorded in the restore point you chose above.

LOCK YOUR SYSTEM

It is important to physically lock your digital exhibit setup. Chapter 3 discussed kiosks for tablets. Securing other components is also important. Most projectors and all-in-one PCs have what are commonly referred to as Kensington lock or k-slot, which is a reinforced tiny hole that allows for a lock and cable system. Smaller components such as the Microsoft Kinect do not have a k-slot. A small lock attached to a cable is an easy way to secure it. Attach the lock to the data cable coming out of the Kinect and then pass a cable through the lock.

Physically locking the components of your digital exhibit is not enough. It is best to restrict access to controls and ports. Controls include on and off switches to displays and projectors. Block access to volume and other control buttons. Restricting this access might require putting the components in special enclosures.

The USB ports, keyboard, and mouse ports need to be restricted as well. Because many of the digital exhibits will run off of computers, it is important to make sure users do not have access to them. This will secure your system from unwanted intruders who may want to access the backend of your system.

7

FUTURE TRENDS

WHAT IS ON THE HORIZON FOR DIGITAL EXHIBITS?

Technology has seen great advancements in recent years. Mobile devices are equipped with better cameras, screens, and processing power. According to the Pew Research Center's Internet & American Life Project, in 2012, 55 percent of adult cell phone users used their cell phones to access the Internet.

The increase in access to information via mobile devices will be important for digital exhibits and collections. Libraries and museums will not be limited to content that is displayed within the exhibit. Patrons will have access to additional content without having to find a PC or laptop to access the information. This additional content will continue to attract patrons. Because information will be hosted in the cloud or on separate servers, it will make it easier for libraries and museums to update and maintain the content.

Advancements in hand-held mobile devices and greater access to online content are not the only things trending that will benefit digital exhibits. Augmented reality (AR) seems to be trending among advertisers in print. This adoption of augmented reality can be very useful in digital exhibits to enhance the user experience. Distinctly created or existing images can be used for patrons to interact with exhibits.

Unlike QR (quick response) codes, which are an array of 2D black-and-white squares generated by a computer, AR image codes can be displayed in a variety of ways. They can be print images, physical objects, or computer-generated symbols. This is important because digital exhibits should be rich with content that is not flat and unappealing. QR codes are not only bland, they are also often overlooked because they only catch the attention of savvy digital users who use them often. An image or object will spark the interest of a visitor and make him or her want to find out more by scanning it using AR. Digital exhibits can greatly benefit from AR.

AR is not perfect and it has limitations and issues. It recent years, there has been much media attention surrounding AR devices, such as Google Glass. Many feel that privacy is a major concern, which can often lead to fears of adopting technologies like AR. Although privacy is a concern and should be addressed, it is not the biggest issue with AR. Looking at it from a technical point of view, there are many more issues. AR technology suffers from the following:

- Image quality
- Object tracking
- Binocular vision
- App standards

Image quality is similar to a cartoon-rendered object. Visually, AR appears more like video game graphic images. The true CGI quality that we experience in a Hollywood movie is not nearly equal to AR. Although the graphics and processing power in mobile devices is much more powerful than it was a few years ago, the processing power is not enough to match those used in CGI movies. Images that are rendered for the AR experience still lack the realism that we would expect in the real world. We are still presented with an object that looks and feels fake and is low-quality CGI. The object does not have the same quality CGI effect that we get from movies. The reason is because the overlays are not videos, but rather animations that are rendered in real time. Much of this limitation is due to the hardware used in our devices.

One of the difficulties in this type of image representation is getting that true-to-life effect without being a rendered video. An example of this is in video games. In gaming, a cut scene will be rendered so well that the object will look as if it were completely real. Once the characters and objects move to actual game play, the effect is less real. You can see that it is a computer-generated effect. This is because the visuals are no longer prerendered. Now it must be done in real time, which takes more processing power. An example of some of the great advances that gaming has made can be seen at http://youtu.be/z0cZin2xDmQ. We can easily see that it is nothing more than a poorly rendered 3D overlay within the real world. These overlays are fine for displaying useful information from text, such as GPS directions, e-mails, or a schedule. But if the goal is to present visual content that is supposed to be as real as the CGI effects in Hollywood movies, then the current AR technology is not there yet.

Object tracking is when a physical object's position is tracked in real time within the physical world. An image is then inserted as an overlay onto the object to create the AR effect. The processing power that mobile devices have often cannot keep track of the object and render the image. The image will experience glitches or lag behind, which causes a ghostly effect. This skipping effect is experienced by the user. Such glitches can ruin the AR experience. In order to remove this undesirable effect, better processing power is needed for mobile devices. Future advancement in both manufactured processor and graphic chips along with improved software will soon fix this issue.

Binocular vision is when the user has difficulty establishing depth. The AR object is often seen out of place and does not have the proper proportion. Many AR applications do a poor job of making sure the depth is correct. Those that do manage to ensure that depth and proportions are correct are limited in the application's scope. The app might be limited to only a certain area or scene that is used for AR.

An example of AR apps that have difficulty with both depth and proportions would be AR furniture apps, such as the Ikea Catalog app. This app allows the user to add virtual furniture to a room. The depth is often incorrect, which gives an unrealistic image of augmented furniture in the room. A user, for instance, may decide to choose a sofa. When placed in the center of the room against a wall, the AR rendering may look fine. But once the user decides to rotate and move the sofa to a corner of the room, the effect is ruined. The app often uses a static image to render a scene. It does not calculate the size of the area, nor does it take into account the angle of view. What the user is left to experience is a flat, unrealistic AR effect.

Another huge problem with AR is the lack of *application standards*. It seems that there are many companies who make AR applications that are used for advertising, research, teaching, productivity, and gaming. Each application is used differently. For those in private industry, the application needs may be for inventory or manufacturing. Some may use it to access information, such as realtors or insurance agents. Advertisers use it to sell products, and gamers for entertainment. Because each image and augmented effect is different, it is nearly impossible to have one AR reader for all these needs. Unlike QR and barcode readers, which either display text or navigate to a URL, companies that use AR will either develop their own proprietary software or use other AR software that is designed for a specific type of need. Companies such as Metaio and Infinity AR have AR applications that can be used by many who wish to incorporate AR. This is very problematic for patrons who want to experience AR. The user often has to install a separate app for each AR company. Imagine having to install a different app for each library or museum you visit. It also becomes difficult for libraries and museums who want to take advantage of this technology. Some may use a company's standard that becomes obsolete. The institution is left having to upgrade or redesign any digital exhibits that used the AR app.

With all of these limitations in AR, it may seem as if it is not quite ready for digital exhibits. The true AR experience of realism may feel like it is not quite there for patrons. One company is trying to change that by bringing a true AR experience that goes beyond the use of tablets and mobile devices. Magic Leap is a mysterious startup company that has gained $542 million in funding by Google and others. The company has also gained the interest of science fiction writer Neal Stephenson, author of *Snow Crash*, who has signed on as their chief futurist.

Magic Leap is taking AR further by projecting augmented objects in the real world. Users will not be tethered to a mobile screen. They will not have to wear oversized head gear to create the effect. Nor will they need to be attached to a larger computer. The company's design will use tiny optic cameras that can be imbeded in glasses. It is similar to Google Glass, but instead of being a heads-up display that is only visible in front view, Magic Leap will project images onto real objects within the real world. Imagine being able to hold your hands out and have a 3D book in them or a tiny 3D elephant. The technology is not available at this time, but the company has gained the support of Google along with others such as chip maker Qualcomm and Legendary Entertainment. Such big investors suggest that Magic Leap is onto something that will be huge in the future.

Magic Leap is not the only company that is pushing the limits of augmented reality. A startup company called castAR promises to use similar technology as Magic Leap. The castAR glasses are equipped with two projectors and a camera for tracking. The system uses a retro-reflective surface to project the AR image. The surface is similar to current AR apps that use an image to display an overlay AR image. The difference for castAR is that it does not use a mobile screen. Although the system requires a retro-reflective area, the effect is quite impressive. A video demonstration can be seen at http://youtu.be/AOI5UW9khoQ.

Visual effects are not the only technology that is on the rise. Digital exhibits will benefit from technologies that incorporate a natural user interface (NUI). NUI is any designed system that uses natural human movement to interact with computers. The motions that navigate or select items in a user interface are common to human interaction. An example would be swiping a hand to turn a web page. The project in chapter 3 used a Microsoft Kinect to add hands-free navigation to an exhibit. Although the Kinect's tracking system is quite impressive, it is limited to only tracking limbs. This limitation creates a user experience that is not quite natural. Turning a page in a virtual book may be done by making a hand-wave gesture. Users are more inclined to naturally grab the corner of the page. Something that feels natural will create a more enjoyable and intuitive experience.

Leap Motion is a company that has invented a product that solves the problem of not having a true NUI. The Leap Motion device not only tracks hand gestures, it also tracks individual digits. Users can actually move their fingers naturally to navigate and interact with virtual objects. The device can track both hands at the same time. With this type of technology, digital exhibits will be able to take advantage of a device that adds a natural feel (figure 7.1). Imagine if patrons were able to interact with a rare book or object that has been rendered in 3D. They would be able to naturally rotate and grab the virtual object. The importance of such technology also extends to preservation. Items such as rare books can be shared both within the library or museum as well as shared with other institutions across distances.

Leap Motion's device has gained support with larger companies such as Hewlett-Packard and Asus, which have incorporated the device into their computers. The technology is also unique in that it does not require any hardware that must be worn by the user. This technology has moved beyond the traditional "Minority Report" gloves (as seen in the Tom Cruise film by the same name) that previous technologies have used in the past.

Where Leap Motion gives the sense of "Minority Report" interaction, Intel wants to bring the entire holographic and seamless hands-free technology right to the user by using more than just the fingertips. A leader in technology, Intel has developed a framework called RealSense, which uses a 3D camera as well as voice recognition. It is very similar to Microsoft Kinect. Unlike the Kinect, RealSense will have the precision of tracking fingers as well, much like the Leap Motion device.

With the 3D camera, users will not only interact hands free, but they will also become part of the environment capturing the world around them. Voice recognition will enhance this interaction with the PC and the world around the user.

Figure 7.1. Athenaeum in Motion with Leap Motion Technology. ***AIM demonstration. Digital Image. The Athenaeum in Motion Project. Binghamton University Libraries. http://library2.binghamton.edu/news/AIM***

How will this benefit digital exhibits? You will be able to create exhibits that go beyond simple visuals and interactions. Imagine being able to have a user insert him- or herself into an interactive exhibit, allowing the user to implement AR to be a part of a rare image or act in an old piece of video footage. Such technology used to be limited to those in Hollywood and advertising. The equipment was not only expensive and bulky, it was also difficult to use. Such technology needed expert users to create some of the simplest images or video.

With RealSense-enabled computers, digital exhibits can take advantage of such technology without the need for expensive hardware or expert users to operate the equipment. Setting up an exhibit will be as easy as setting up a computer and creating content for it.

RealSense will also allow you to bring physical objects to your digital exhibit. Imagine a digital exhibit on rare garments of the seventeenth century. Suppose the exhibit wanted users to be able to virtually try on the outfits. The 3D RealSense camera will allow users to create a 3D model scan of themselves. This 3D model can then be used with the virtual outfits from an exhibit. Users might also enjoy having a 3D printed figurine of themselves. With other innovators in 3D printing, such as HP Multi Jet Fusion technology, users will be able to print a 3D object in a matter of minutes.

Intel's RealSense is already finding its way onto tablets, two-in-one laptops, as well as all-in-one PCs. Companies such as Dell, Acer, and Asus are already working on incorporating RealSense into their Windows computers. RealSense is also making its way into non-Windows PCs as well. Acer's Chromebook 15 will have RealSense technology.

One other trending technology for digital exhibits is haptic technology. It is the technology that is used to create tactile feedback. It recreates the sense of touch by using force, motion, or vibrations. Such technology is not new; the gaming industry has already developed hardware to enhance gaming. Vests with force feedback were developed in the 1990s. Gamers would wear a vest that was fitted with speakers to create a haptic effect using sound. For instance, if a gamer was struck in a boxing game, the vest would give force feedback to the chest.

Haptic technology has moved beyond wearable vests that use speakers to create feedback. Technological innovators like the Walt Disney Company are working on tactile feedback that uses air. Disney's Aireal is a low-cost and scalable technology that allows it to launch projectiles of air in midair. Almost entirely made from 3D printed parts, the Aireal would be a great tool for digital exhibits.

Combined with AR, users will not only be able to visually experience 3D objects, but they will feel and sense them as well. A digital exhibit has the potential to go beyond visuals and add the sense of touch. Aireal can be strategically placed around an exhibit to create all sorts of effects. Imagine creating an exhibit of rare birds. Visitors could be surrounded by virtual 3D birds that will not only fly around them, but where they can also feel the excitement of actually being in the room with them. Tiny rings of air that are used in a vortex would interact with the users.

Much of the interactive technology in the past decade has made huge advancements. Even technology that seems out of the realm of reality has regained new interest. Technology such as virtual reality has experienced a whole new enthusiasm with the inventions of the Oculus Rift technology company and is gaining large support. Users are finding themselves in much more immersive worlds, and they are the type of worlds that digital exhibits can greatly benefit from.

The inventions of Microsoft Kinect and Leap Motion also have helped to create this new and exciting world of immersion. They continue to remain innovative tools where developers are creating exciting new applications that engage users. The Kinect is still being used by developers to invent unique and useful applications and systems.

Microsoft's experimental design RoomAlive is one such invention. This interesting system uses several projectors and Kinects, which are placed in high places around a room. Each projector and Kinect is carefully calculated and placed overhead. The projectors and Kinects create an AR space that projects objects onto the real world. The Kinects are used to track users in real time. Tracking the users allows the Kinects to create a system that users can interact with inside the room, bringing us closer to the Star Trek Holodeck of the future. All of these exciting technologies will soon be available, so start planning for them in your own digital exhibits!

Small startup companies such as Leap Motion and Magic Leap are bringing us new and exciting technologies that play to our sense of touch and sight. They are helping to usher in a new era of AR. Their rapid growth in research and development is gaining the interest of companies such as Microsoft, Hewlett-Packard, Google, Apple, and

Facebook. This interest is leading to support from them. Soon these exciting technologies will easily be available for you to use and incorporate into your own digital exhibits. The exhibits that you will create will go beyond what we could only have imagined up until now.

RECOMMENDED READING

BOOKS

Kalfatovic, Martin R. *Creating a Winning Online Exhibition: A Guide for Libraries, Archives, and Museums*. Chicago: American Library Association, 2002. Print.

Thiel, Sarah Goodwin. *Build It Once: A Basic Primer for the Creation of Online Exhibitions*. Lanham, MD: Scarecrow, 2007. Print.

ARTICLES

Ajmi, Ayyoub. "The DIY Digital Exhibition Experience at Tarrant County College." *Journal of Library Innovation* 5.1 (2014): 98–126. Web.

"Best Mobile Gadgets | Smart Phones Tablets—Consumer Reports." *Consumer Reports*. June 2013. http://consumerreports.org/cro/magazine/2013/08/8-trends-in-mobile-devices/index.htm. Web.

Capelle, Quentin. "UltraHaptics Uses Ultrasound to Bring Tactile Feedback to Digital Touchscreens." *L'Atelier*. 24 Oct. 2013. http://www.atelier.net/en/trends/articles/ultrahaptics-uses-ultrasound-bring-tactile-feedback-digital-touchscreens_424813. Web.

Dibble, Anand. "3 Biggest Augmented Reality Problems and How to Fix Them." *Brainberry Global*. 25 July 2014. http://brainberryglobal.com/3-biggest-problems-facing-augmented-reality-today-fix/. Web.

Fulton, Will. "Author Neal Stephenson Joins AR Upstart Magic Leap as Chief Futurist." *Digital Trends*. 20 Dec. 2014. http://www.digitaltrends.com/gaming/author-neal-stephenson-joins-ar-upstart-magic-leap-chief-futurist/. Web.

Gannes, Liz, and Peter Kafka. "Look Who Else Is Joining Google to Back Magic Leap, the Secret 'Augmented Reality' Startup (Updated)." *Recode*. 20 Oct. 2014. http://recode.net/2014/10/20/look-who-else-is-joining-google-to-back-magic-leap-the-secret-augmented-reality-startup/. Web.

Hughes, Neil. "Apple's Haptic Touch Feedback Concept Uses Actuators, Senses Force on IPhone, IPad." *AppleInsider*. 22 Mar. 2012. http://appleinsider.com/articles/12/03/22/apples_haptic_touch_feedback_concept_uses_actuators_senses_force_on_iphone_ipad. Web.

Lambson, Brice. "Image Resizer for Windows." *CodePlex*. 31 Mar. 2014. https://imageresizer.codeplex.com/. Web.

McNicoll, Arion, and Jenny Soffel. "'Feel' Objects in Thin Air: The Future of Touch Technology." *CNN*. 29 Oct. 2013. http://www.cnn.com/2013/10/29/tech/innovation/feel-objects-in-thin-air/. Web.

Parrish, Kevin. "4 Cool New Haptic Feedback and Touchscreen Technologies." *Tom's Hardware*. 12 Mar. 2014. http://www.tomshardware.com/news/feedback-tactile-heptic-touch-fujitsu,26244.html. Web.

"Repurposed Laptop Project: Home." Tarrant County College. n.d. http://libguides.tccd.edu/nedigitalexhibit. Web.

Russell, Mallory. "11 Amazing Augmented Reality Ads." *Business Insider*. 28 Jan. 2012. http://www.businessinsider.com/11-amazing-augmented-reality-ads-2012-1. Web.

Smith, Aaron. "Cell Phones, Social Media and Campaign 2014." *Pew Research Centers Internet American Life Project RSS*. 25 June 2012. http://www.pewinternet.org/2014/11/03/cell-phones-social-media-and-campaign-2014/. Web.

WEBSITES

"Aireal: Interactive Tactile Experiences in Free Air." Disney Research. n.d. http://www.disneyresearch.com/project/aireal/. Web.

"The AR Magic Book Project." Binghamton University Libraries. n.d. http://library2.binghamton.edu/news/armb/. Web.

"The Athenaeum in Motion Project." Binghamton University Libraries. n.d. http://library2.binghamton.edu/news/aim/. Web.

"Audacity: Free Audio Editor and Recorder." Audacity. n.d. http://audacity.sourceforge.net/. Web.

"Autodesk 123D—Free 3D Modeling Software, 3D Models, DIY Projects, Personal Fabrication Tools." Autodesk Inc. n.d. http://www.123dapp.com/. Web.

"Binghamton University—Binghamton University: Art Museum." Binghamton University Art Museum. n.d. http://www.binghamton.edu/art-museum/. Web.

"Capture, Edit, and Share Your Ideas with TechSmith Camtasia." Techsmith Corp. n.d. http://www.techsmith.com/camtasia.html. Web.

"CastAR Glasses" *CastAR*. Technical Illusions. n.d. http://technicalillusions.com/portfolio_page/castar-glasses/. Web.

"FileMaker Go 13." Filemaker Inc. n.d. http://www.filemaker.com/products/filemaker-go/whats-new.html. Web.

"GIMP 2.8." *GIMP*. n.d. http://www.gimp.org/. Web.

"HMRC—Exhibit Snapshot." n.p., n.d. http://digital.houstonlibrary.org/virtual/faces-places/. Web.

"The Infinity Augmented Reality Platform. InfinityAR. n.d. http://www.infinityar.com/. Web.

"Intel® WiDi and Intel® Pro Wireless Display." Intel. n.d. http://www.intel.com/content/www/us/en/architecture-and-technology/intel-pro-wireless-display.html. Web.

"Kinect for Windows." Microsoft. n.d. http://www.microsoft.com/en-us/kinectforwindows/. Web.

"Leap Motion." Leap Motion Inc. n.d. https://www.leapmotion.com/. Web.

"Magic Leap." Magic Leap Inc. n.d. https://www.leapmotion.com/. Web.

"Metaio." Metaio. n.d. http://www.metaio.com/. Web.

"Microsoft Expression Changes." Microsoft. n.d. http://www.microsoft.com/expression/eng/. Web.

"Microsoft Research HD View." Microsoft Research. n.d. http://research.microsoft.com/en-us/um/redmond/groups/ivm/HDView/. Web.

"Microsoft Research Image Composite Editor (ICE)." Microsoft Research. n.d. http://research.microsoft.com/en-us/um/redmond/projects/ice/. Web.

"Moovly." *Home*. Moovly. n.d. https://www.moovly.com/. Web.

"Omeka." *Omeka Blog RSS*. Roy Rosenzweig Center for History and New Media, George Mason University. n.d. http://omeka.org/. Web.

"Open Exhibits | Multitouch, Multiuser Software for Museums." Open Exhibits. n.p., n.d. http://openexhibits.org/. Web.

"Prezi." n.d. http://prezi.com/. Web.

"Projects: Timetraveler." *Timetraveler*. 4 May 2014. http://timetraveler.berlin/. Web.

"RoomAlive—Microsoft Research." Microsoft Research. n.d. http://research.microsoft.com/en-us/projects/roomalive/. Web.

"Smithsonian X 3D." Smithsonian Institute. n.d. http://3d.si.edu/. Web.

"Touchless Touch." *Turn Any Surface into a Touch Screen*. RobSmithDev. n.d. http://www.touchlesstouch.com/. Web.

"Ubi Interactive Touchscreen." Ubi-Interactive. n.d. http://www.ubi-interactive.com/. Web.

INDEX

ABOUT THE AUTHOR

Juan Denzer is a library systems specialist at Binghamton University in Binghamton, New York. He is a graduate of Binghamton University, where he received a bachelor's degree in computer science in 2004. He is currently working on his master's degree in library and information science at Buffalo University online.

Before working in the library, he worked in the private sector as a systems administrator and developer. He has developed several custom applications for companies that include an automated security entry system for a twenty-four-hour gym, a fully automated Ebay listing system, and an inventory loading system for a small trucking company that supports the Raymond Corporation in Greene, New York.

He has taken his vast knowledge of computer systems and developing software to the library community. He uses it to educate and train faculty and staff and also uses his passion for technology and libraries to give national presentations across the country. Some of the library conferences that he has presented at include Computers in Libraries, IDS Project, and Internet Librarian. He was also invited to speak at the ELI Educause annual meeting for his work with the Leap Motion device and Rare Books. He is currently working on an exciting new invention he created called the AR Magic Book, which will help present digital collections in libraries and museums in a whole new way (http://library2.binghamton.edu/news/ARMB/).

CPSIA information can be obtained at www.ICGtesting.com
Printed in the USA
BVOW08s2258170715

409182BV00001B/2/P